FOLENS IT
Keyboard Skills 3

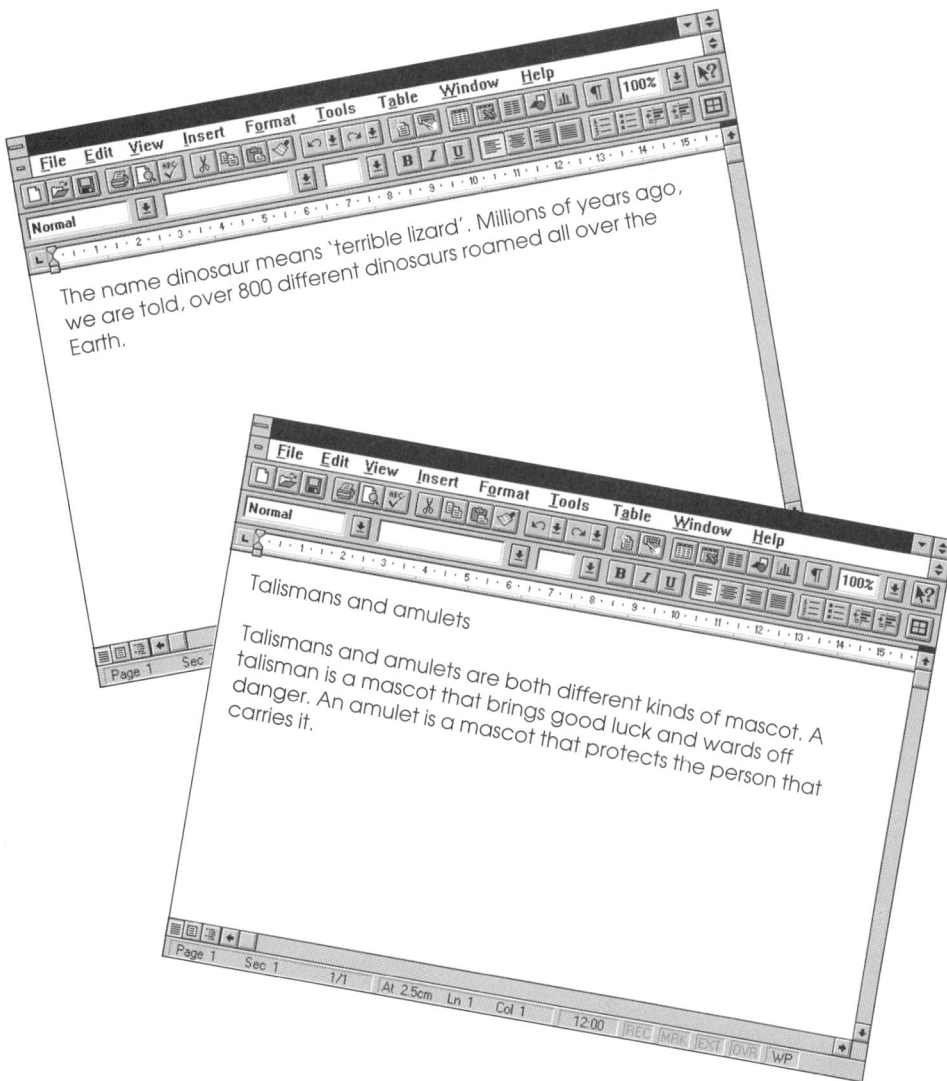

File Edit View Insert Format Tools Table Window Help 100%

Normal

The name dinosaur means 'terrible lizard'. Millions of years ago, we are told, over 800 different dinosaurs roamed all over the Earth.

Page 1 Sec

File Edit View Insert Format Tools Table Window Help

Normal

Talismans and amulets

Talismans and amulets are both different kinds of mascot. A talisman is a mascot that brings good luck and wards off danger. An amulet is a mascot that protects the person that carries it.

Page 1 Sec 1 1/1 At 2.5cm Ln 1 Col 1 12.00 REC MRK EXT OVR WP

Folens
Publishers

HOLCOMBE BROOK
C.P. SCHOOL
LONGSIGHT ROAD
RAMSBOTTOM, LANCS.

Elizabeth Price

Contents

Acknowledgements

Folens allows photocopying of pages marked 'copiable page' for educational use, providing that this use is within the confines of the purchasing institution. Copiable pages should not be declared in any return in respect of any photocopying licence.

Folens books are protected by international copyright laws. All rights are reserved. The copyright of all materials in this book, except where otherwise stated, remains the property of the publisher and authors. No part of this publication may be reproduced, stored in a retrieval system, or transmitted, in any form or by any means, for whatever purpose, without the written permission of Folens Limited.

This resource may be used in a variety of ways. However, it is not intended that teachers or children should write directly into the book itself.

Elizabeth Price hereby asserts her moral rights to be identified as the author of this work in accordance with the Copyright, Designs and Patents Act 1988.

Editor: Ian Jenkins   Layout artist: Margaret Tindall
Cover design: Kim Ashby/Two's Company

©1997 Folens Limited, on behalf of the author.

Every effort has been made to contact copyright holders of material used in this book. If any have been overlooked, we will be pleased to make any necessary arrangements.

Elizabeth Price wishes to thank:
    The head teacher and children of Llangurig C P School, Powys, for taking part in the pilot scheme.
    The head teacher, staff and children of Cefn Llys Primary School, Llandrindod Wells, Powys, for their enthusiastic adoption of Keyboard Skills.
    Her husband Jim for his encouragement and advice throughout the writing of this book.

First published 1997 by Folens Limited, Dunstable and Dublin.
Folens Limited, Albert House, Apex Business Centre, Boscombe Road, Dunstable, LU5 4RL, England.

ISBN 1 85276369-8
Printed in Singapore by Craft Print.

Introduction

This book provides activities that blend keyboard skills with word-processing activities to enable children to consolidate and develop the keyboard skills learned in *Folens IT – Keyboard Skills Book 1* and *Book 2*.

All of the activities in *Book 3* require the children to key in and manipulate text in various ways. The word-processing software referred to throughout the book is *Microsoft Word for Windows*, although other word-processing software could also be used.

The activities progress from simple manipulation of text to adding borders and shading. Simple instructions are given at the beginning of each section. The instructions are in clear, straightforward language, with technical terms kept to a minimum.

In all these activities, the children are in control, although some teacher support may be necessary in some cases. Each section provides practice of keyboard skills and word-processing in the widest context. The level of English required is well within the scope of primary school children.

Folens IT – Keyboard Skills Book 3 provides in-depth practice of the basic keyboard skills developed in *Book 1* and *Book 2*, as well as developing these skills by applying them to word-processing. A child who completes *Book 3* successfully may proudly claim to be proficient in the basic skills of word-processing.

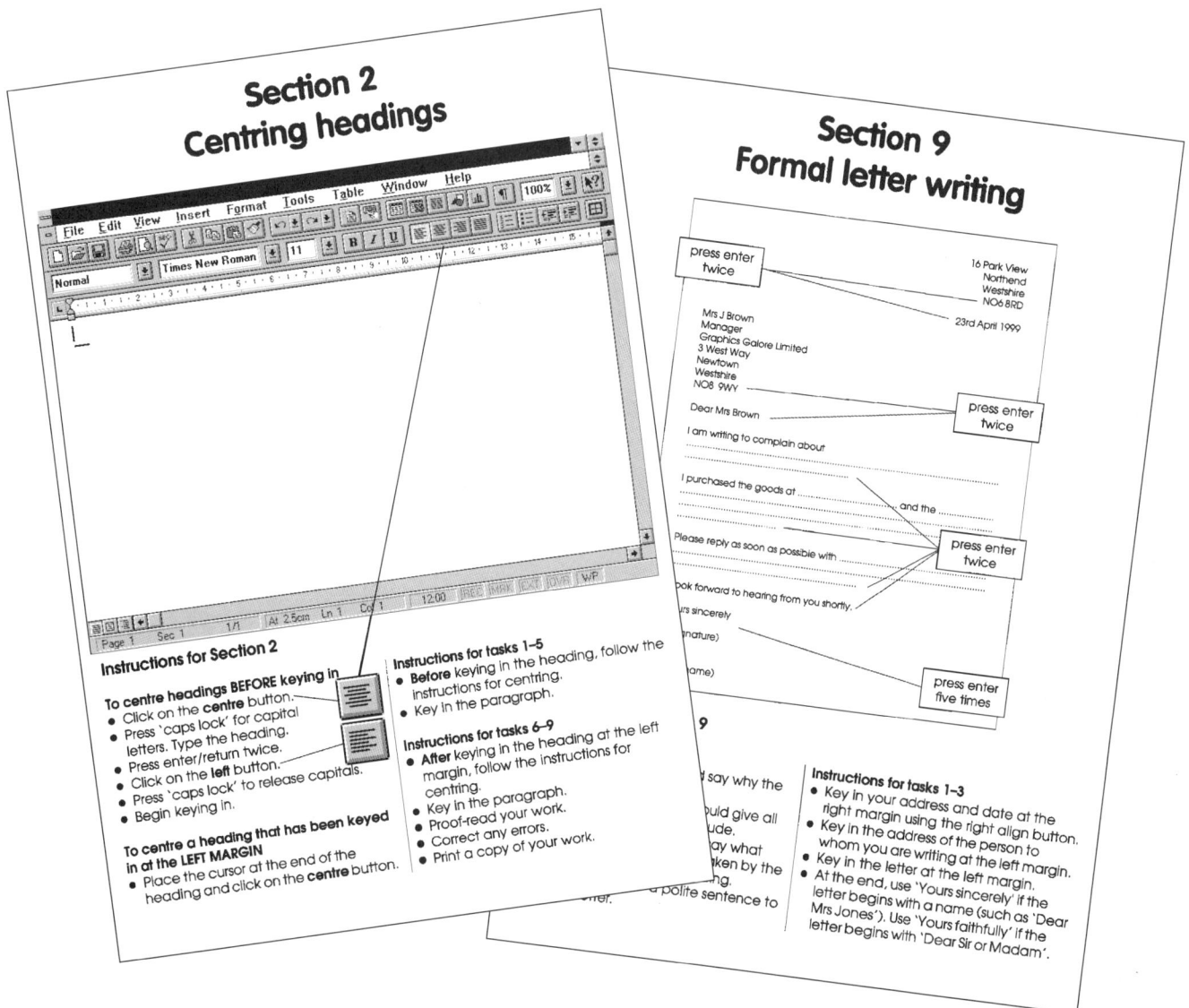

Section 2
Centring headings

Instructions for Section 2

To centre headings BEFORE keying in
- Click on the **centre** button.
- Press 'caps lock' for capital letters. Type the heading.
- Press enter/return twice.
- Click on the **left** button.
- Press 'caps lock' to release capitals.
- Begin keying in.

To centre a heading that has been keyed in at the LEFT MARGIN
- Place the cursor at the end of the heading and click on the **centre** button.

Instructions for tasks 1–5
- Before keying in the heading, follow the instructions for centring.
- Key in the paragraph.

Instructions for tasks 6–9
- After keying in the heading at the left margin, follow the instructions for centring.
- Key in the paragraph.
- Proof-read your work.
- Correct any errors.
- Print a copy of your work.

Section 9
Formal letter writing

press enter twice

16 Park View
Northend
Westshire
NO6 8RD

23rd April 1999

Mrs J Brown
Manager
Graphics Galore Limited
3 West Way
Newtown
Westshire
NO8 9WY

press enter twice

Dear Mrs Brown

I am writing to complain about

I purchased the goods at

and the

press enter twice

Please reply as soon as possible with

ook forward to hearing from you shortly.

rs sincerely

(ignature)

ame)

press enter five times

... say why the
... uld give all
... ude.
... ay what
... ken by the
... ng.
... a polite sentence to
... er.

Instructions for tasks 1–3
- Key in your address and date at the right margin using the right align button.
- Key in the address of the person to whom you are writing at the left margin.
- Key in the letter at the left margin.
- At the end, use 'Yours sincerely' if the letter begins with a name (such as 'Dear Mrs Jones'). Use 'Yours faithfully' if the letter begins with 'Dear Sir or Madam'.

The word-processor screen

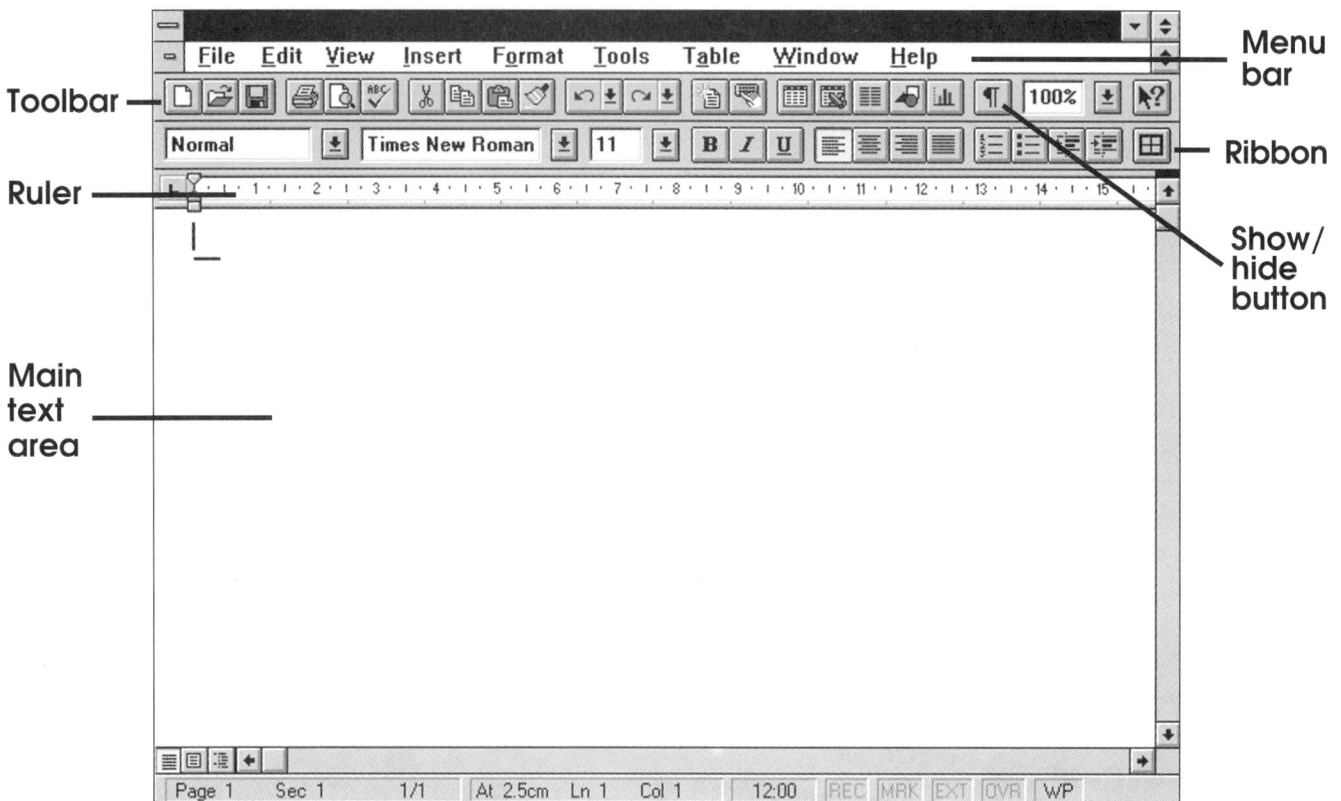

Toolbar — [toolbar icons]

Ruler — [ruler]

Main text area —

Menu bar — File Edit View Insert Format Tools Table Window Help

Ribbon — Normal Times New Roman 11 B I U

Show/ hide button

Page 1 Sec 1 1/1 At 2.5cm Ln 1 Col 1 12:00 REC MRK EXT OVR WP

Using the features of the word-processor

This is the main word-processor screen that is referred to throughout this book. It is the main screen from *Microsoft Word*, although other word-processing software uses similar features.

All of the features shown on this picture of the screen can be activated using the mouse. If the toolbar, ribbon and ruler are not displayed, click on **View** in the menu bar. A pull-down menu will appear. Click on **Toolbars**. A box will then appear with a choice of toolbars that can be used on screen.

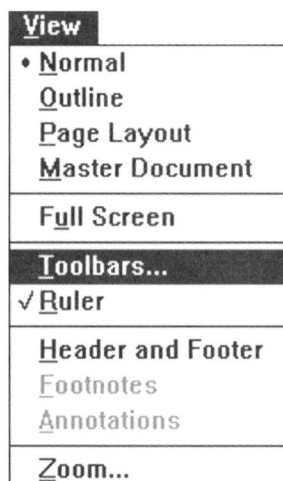

View
- • **Normal**
- **Outline**
- **Page Layout**
- **Master Document**

Full Screen

Toolbars...
√**Ruler**

Header and Footer
Footnotes
Annotations

Zoom...

Using symbols with word-processing

Key in some text, then click on the show/hide button on the right side of the toolbar at the top of the screen.

The following symbols will appear in your text:
- ● paragraph symbols ¶ where you have pressed enter/return
- ● dots where you have pressed the space bar
- ● arrows where you have pressed the tab key.

These symbols are useful for checking the spacing between lines, words and punctuation.

Click on the show/hide button again to turn off the symbols.

Presentation and layout of documents

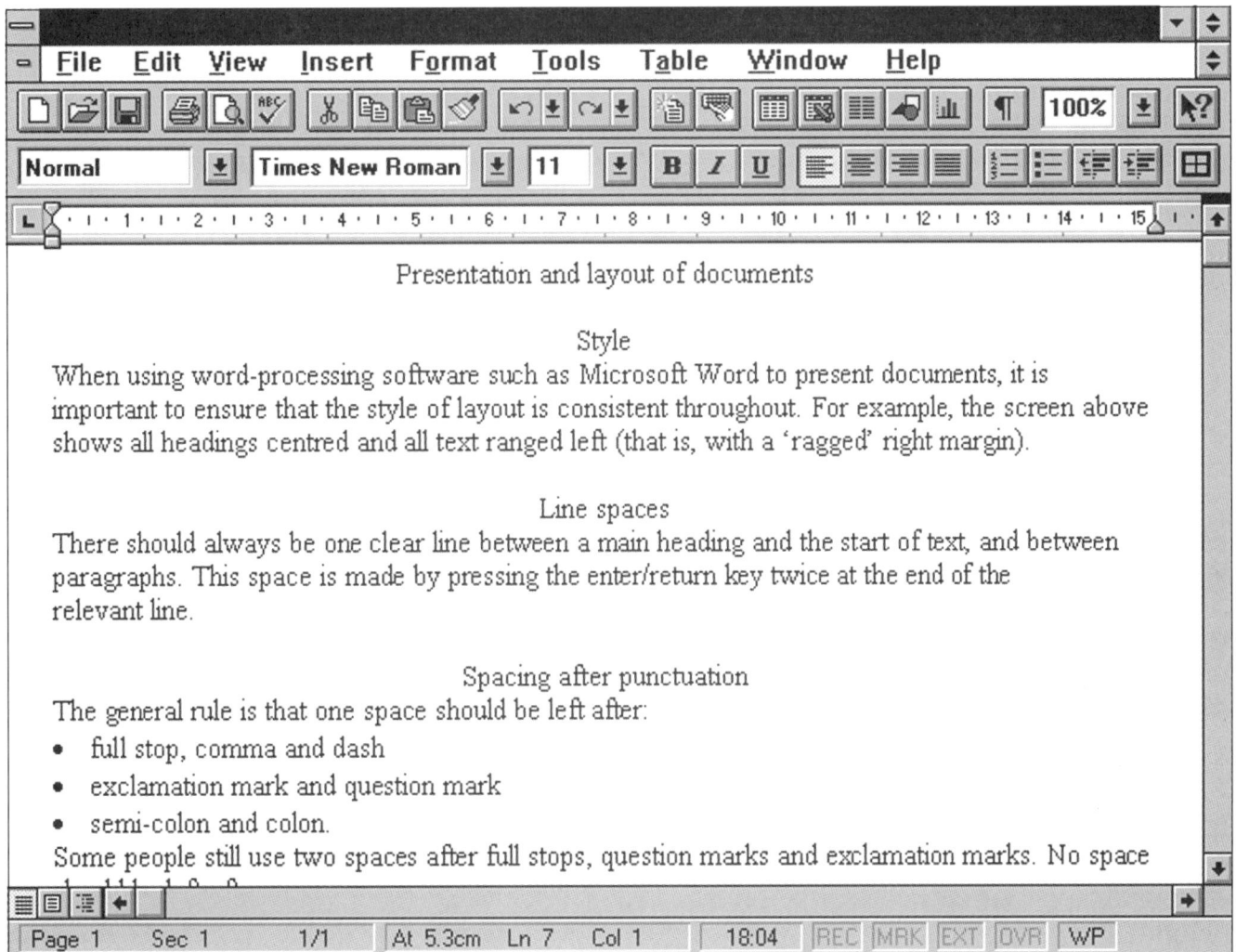

[Screen image of Microsoft Word document]

File Edit View Insert Format Tools Table Window Help

Normal | Times New Roman | 11

Presentation and layout of documents

Style
When using word-processing software such as Microsoft Word to present documents, it is important to ensure that the style of layout is consistent throughout. For example, the screen above shows all headings centred and all text ranged left (that is, with a 'ragged' right margin).

Line spaces
There should always be one clear line between a main heading and the start of text, and between paragraphs. This space is made by pressing the enter/return key twice at the end of the relevant line.

Spacing after punctuation
The general rule is that one space should be left after:
- full stop, comma and dash
- exclamation mark and question mark
- semi-colon and colon.
Some people still use two spaces after full stops, question marks and exclamation marks. No space

Page 1 Sec 1 1/1 At 5.3cm Ln 7 Col 1 18:04 REC MRK EXT OVR WP

Style

When using word-processing software such as *Microsoft Word* to present documents, it is important to ensure that the style of layout is consistent throughout. For example, the screen above shows all headings centred and all text ranged left (that is, with a 'ragged' right margin).

Line spaces

There should always be one clear line between a main heading and the start of text, and between paragraphs. This space is made by pressing the enter/ return key twice at the end of the relevant line.

Spacing after punctuation

The general rule is that one space should be left after:
- full stop, comma and dash
- exclamation mark and question mark
- semi-colon and colon.
Some people use two spaces after full stops, question marks and exclamation marks. No space should be left after:
- opening speech mark
- opening parenthesis
- hyphen.

There are no hard and fast rules, but these guidelines are in keeping with standard modern practice. **Consistency** is the key when word processing.

Basics of word-processing

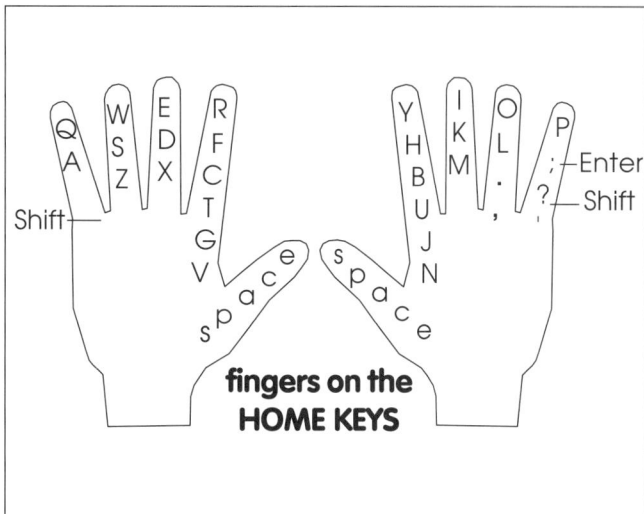

fingers on the HOME KEYS

To key in text
● The diagram at the top of this page shows the finger positions for keying in.
● Children should be competent at keying in before attempting the word-processing activities in this book.

To highlight text to make changes
● Place your hand on the mouse, with your index finger resting lightly on the left button.
● **Move** the mouse until the pointer I is to the left of the words or letters you want to highlight.
● **Press** and **hold** the left mouse button.
● **Drag** the pointer I across the text from left to right by moving the mouse.
● **Release** the button. Your text is now **highlighted**.

To highlight whole lines, paragraphs and pages
● The mouse pointer changes to a ◁ when you place it in the left margin.
● **Click once** to highlight the line.
● **Click twice** to highlight the paragraph.
● **Click three times** to highlight the whole page.

To delete text
● **Highlight** text to be changed.
● **Move** the mouse arrow until it rests on the **cut** button ✂ in the toolbar.
● **Click** the left mouse button once.
● Key in the correction.
● Alternatively, use the arrow keys to move the cursor to the right of the text you want to delete, then press the backspace/delete key.

To insert text
● **Move** the mouse pointer to where you want to insert the text.
● **Click** the left button once.
● Key in the text.
● Adjust the spacing if necessary.
● Alternatively, use the arrow keys to move the cursor to where you want to insert the text, then key in the changes.

Additional function keys
● Most keyboards contain a set of six keys at the right of the main keyboard:

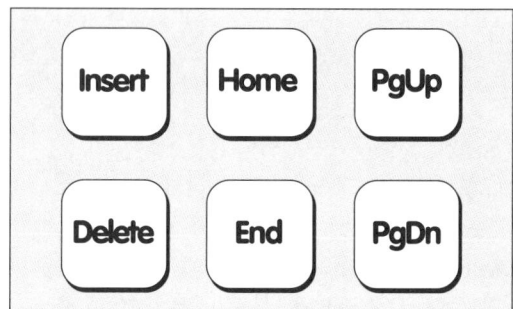

● The **Insert** key: press this once to allow you to key in text as normal. Press the key again to allow you to type over the top of existing text.
● The **Delete** key: deletes from left to right.
● The **Home** and **End** keys: press these keys with the control key to move to the beginning or end of a document.
● The **Page Up** and **Page Down** keys: move the screen up or down a page.

Section 1
Inserting and deleting text
and making changes

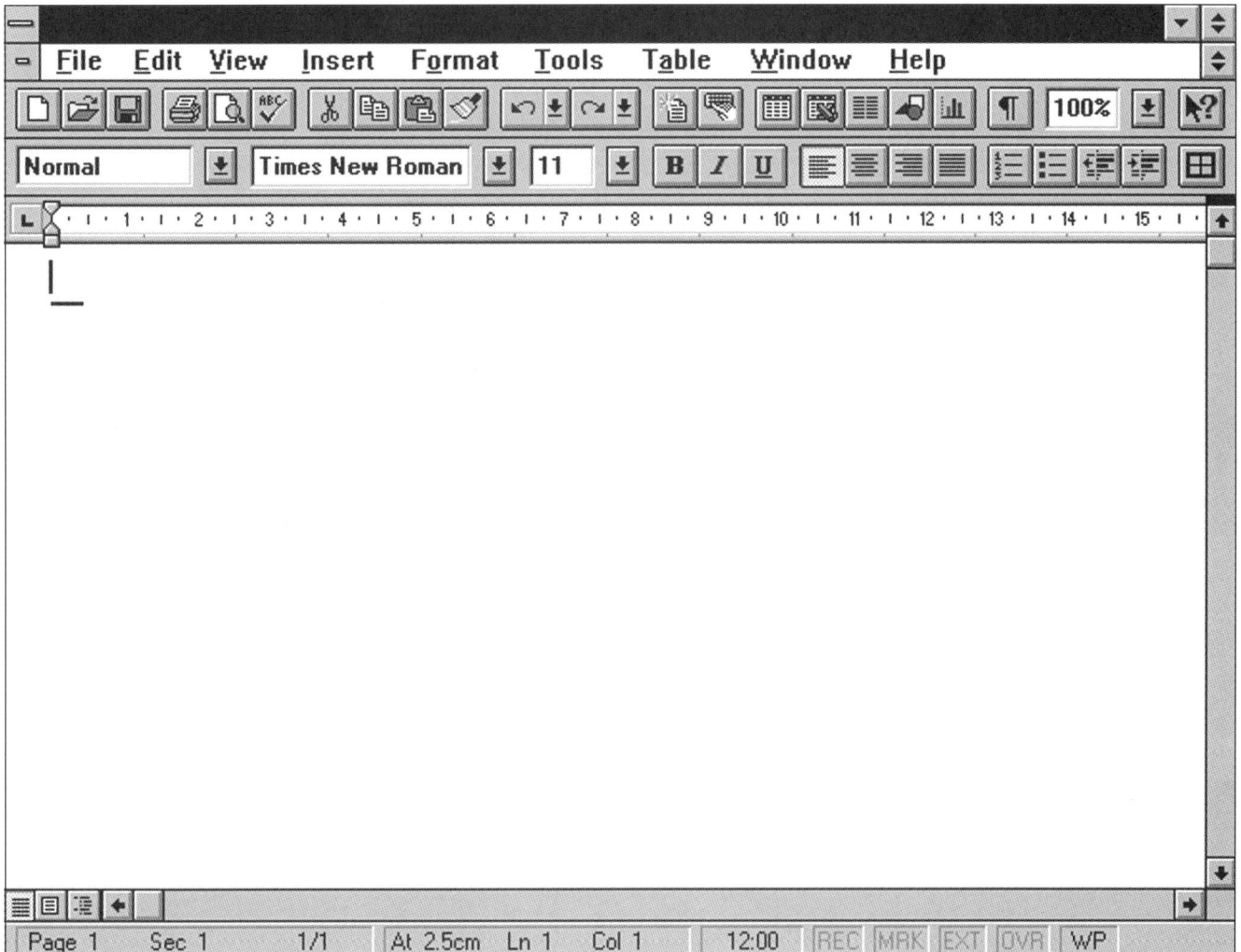

Normal | Times New Roman | 11

```
File    Edit    View    Insert    Format    Tools    Table    Window    Help
```

`·1·1·2·1·3·1·4·1·5·1·6·1·7·1·8·1·9·1·10·1·11·1·12·1·13·1·14·1·15·1·`

Page 1   Sec 1   1/1   At 2.5cm   Ln 1   Col 1   12:00   REC MRK EXT OVR WP

Instructions for Section 1

- Key in the task before making the changes.

- Carry out the changes at the end of the task by:
  - using the arrow keys and backspace/ delete key to change single letters
  - using the mouse to change whole words.

- Read through your work for any errors (proof-reading).

- Adjust the punctuation and spacing if necessary. Key in any corrections.

- Print a copy of your work.

Section 1 – task 1

The name dinosaur means 'terrible lizard'. Millions of years ago, we are told, over 800 different dinosaurs roamed all over the Earth.

The fiercest of all the known dinosaurs was Tyrannosaurus Rex. Its name means 'king of the tyrant reptiles'. It lived about 70 million years ago and weighed around 8 tonnes. It was 15 metres long and 6 metres tall when standing upright. In addition to being absolutely enormous, it had razor sharp teeth which were 15 centimetres long. It also had thick curved talons which it used for killing its prey and tearing it apart. Although it had very powerful legs, it was too heavy to move quickly, so the faster its prey could run the greater their chance of survival.

The mystery of why the dinosaurs became extinct has never been solved. The two main theories are a change in vegetation or a change in the Earth's climate. Whatever the reason, seeing the film 'Jurassic Park' made me quite thankful that something did happen to wipe the dinosaurs off the face of the Earth!

Changes

1. **First paragraph, second sentence**
   Delete the words (and commas)
   ', we are told,'.

2. **Second paragraph, first sentence**
   Delete the word 'known' and insert the word 'ancient'.

3. **Second paragraph, last sentence**
   Insert the word 'very' before 'quickly'.

4. **Last paragraph, last sentence**
   Delete the word 'quite'.

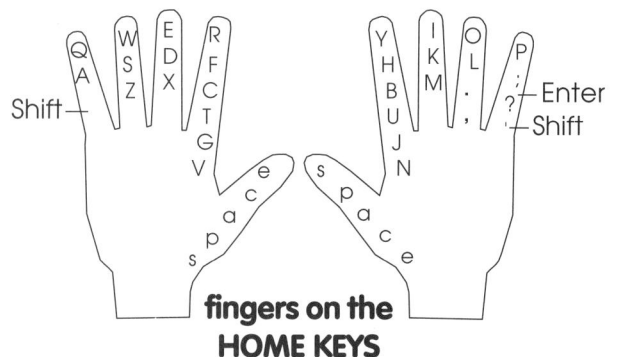

fingers on the
HOME KEYS

Section 1 – task 2

As I browsed through the collection of books that my family has gathered over the years, I realised that 'unusual happenings' and stories of strange and interesting creatures were big favourites. Our books range from myths and legends to amazing tales of the wonders of the world. As I looked through these old favourites, I became interested and started to read.

Many of these stories are fantasy and are not to be believed. Indeed, some people say that none of the stories can be believed. However, the same people often read their horoscopes every day in the newspapers, because they want to find out what fate might have in store for them.

It can be a wonderful fantasy to dream about what might happen in the future. People dream in different ways about what might make them happy, but just reading books and stories brings a great deal of happiness to many people.

Changes

1. **First paragraph, last sentence**
   Delete the word 'looked' and insert the word 'glanced'.

2. **First paragraph, last sentence**
   Delete the word 'started' and insert the word 'began'.

3. **Second paragraph, last sentence**
   Delete the words 'in the newspapers'.

4. **Third paragraph, second sentence**
   Delete the word 'many' and insert the words 'lots of'.

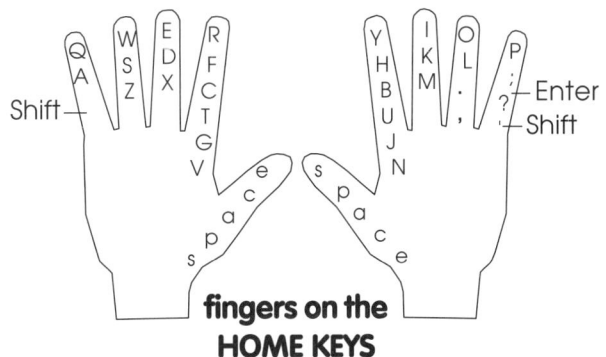

Section 1 – task 3

The Sahara Desert is the largest desert in the world and it is still growing! It measures about 9 million square kilometres and is said to be growing at a rate of 1.5 million hectares every year. This is equal to four football pitches every minute! The desert stretches across north Africa, all the way from the Atlantic Ocean to the Red Sea.

From the ancient rock pictures discovered in Algeria many years ago, we know that the Sahara Desert was not always a sandy waste land. It was once a green fertile plain with many different trees, plants and animals. Now, however, there is almost no rainfall or surface water. There are some underground rivers that sometimes find their way to the surface. When this happens an oasis is formed.

The Sahara has the biggest sand dunes of all the world's deserts, the largest of which can be up to 430 metres high. The Sahara is also the home of the desert locust, which is said to be able to fly further than any other insect. Huge swarms of these locusts fly 3,200 kilometres in a great circle around the desert.

Changes

1. **First paragraph, second sentence**
   Delete the word 'about' and insert the word 'almost'.

2. **Second paragraph, first sentence**
   Delete the words 'many years ago'.

3. **Third paragraph, first sentence**
   Delete the word 'biggest' and insert the word 'highest'.

4. **Third paragraph, last sentence**
   Insert the word 'can' before the word 'fly'.

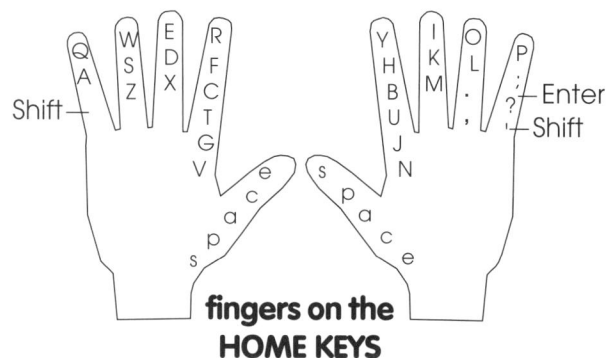

fingers on the HOME KEYS

Section 1 – task 4

Some of the gods and goddesses worshipped by the Ancient Greeks were beautiful and powerful supernatural beings. Others were hideous monsters, half human and half beast, or a nasty combination of two or more animals.

Perhaps the story of the Gorgons, three sisters who had snakes growing out of their heads, is one of the best known. The Gorgon sisters were so hideous, that anyone who met them face-to-face was turned to stone with horror.

Medusa, the most famous of the sisters, had been very beautiful. The goddess Athena thought she was too beautiful and in a fit of jealous rage changed her into a hideous monster. Perseus, a Greek hero, was given the terrible task of cutting off Medusa's head. To help him do the job, the goddess Athena gave him a shining shield and a helmet that would make him invisible.

While he was invisible, Perseus crept up on Medusa as she slept. Knowing he would be turned to stone if he looked her in the face, he used the shining surface of his shield to reflect her image. He then managed to cut off her head. He went home with Medusa's head in a bag and triumphantly claimed his bride.

Changes

1. **Second paragraph, first sentence**
   Delete the word 'Perhaps'. Change capital letters and spacing.

2. **Third paragraph, first sentence**
   Delete the words 'had been' and insert the word 'was'.

3. **Fourth paragraph, third sentence**
   Insert the words 'with difficulty' after the word 'managed'.

4. **Fourth paragraph, last sentence**
   Delete the word 'triumphantly'.

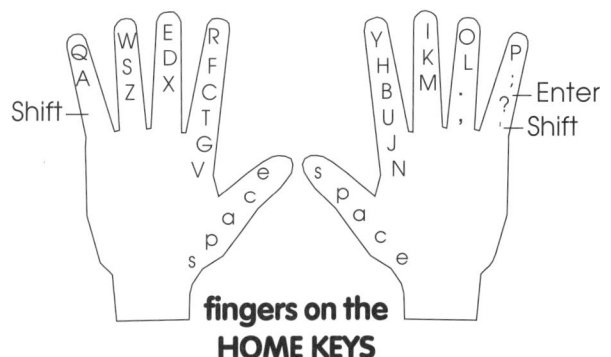

fingers on the
HOME KEYS

Section 2
Centring headings

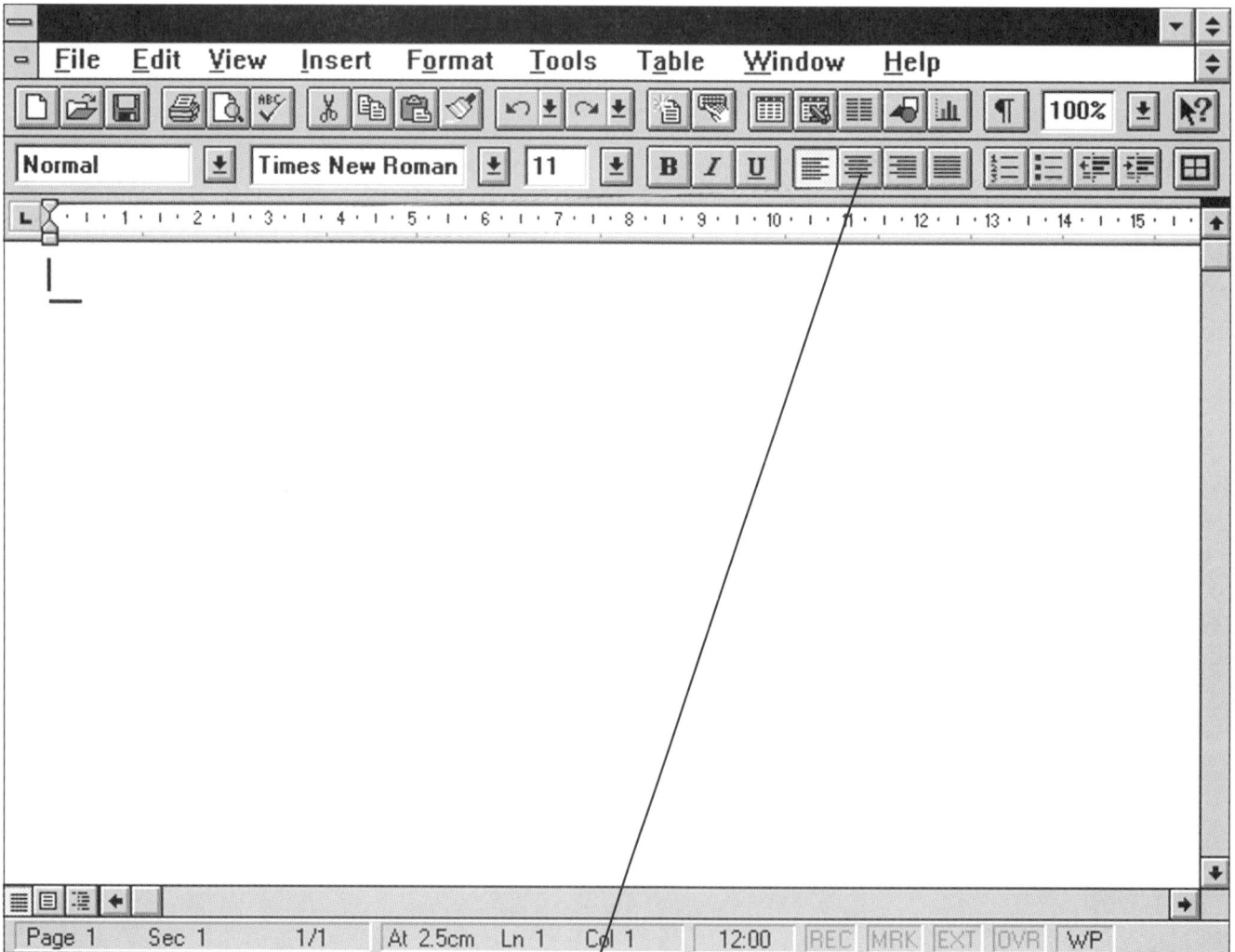

```
 ┌─────────────────────────────────────────────────────────────────────────┐
 │ ▼ ▲                                                                       │
 │  File   Edit   View   Insert   Format   Tools   Table   Window   Help  ▲  │
 │ [□][☞][🖫][🖨][🔍][✓] [✂][📋][📋][🖌] [↶][↷] [📄][🖉][▦][▦][▤][◢][📊][¶][100%][±][▶?] │
 │ Normal      [±] Times New Roman [±] 11 [±] [B][I][U] [≡][≡][≡][≡] [≣][≣][⮒][⮓][⊞] │
 │ L ·1·1·2·1·3·1·4·1·5·1·6·1·7·1·8·1·9·1·10·1·11·1·12·1·13·1·14·1·15·1·     │
 │  |                                                                        │
 │  ‾                                                                        │
 │                                                                           │
 │                                                                           │
 │                                                                           │
 │                                                                           │
 │                                                                           │
 │                                                                           │
 │                                                                           │
 │                                                                           │
 │                                                                           │
 │                                                                           │
 │                                                                           │
 │ [≡][≣][⮓][←]                                                           → │
 │ [Page 1] [Sec 1] [1/1] [At 2.5cm][Ln 1][Col 1] [12:00] [REC][MRK][EXT][OVR][WP] │
 └─────────────────────────────────────────────────────────────────────────┘
```

Instructions for Section 2

To centre headings BEFORE keying in
- Click on the **centre** button.
- Press 'caps lock' for capital letters. Type the heading.
- Press enter/return twice.
- Click on the **left** button.
- Press 'caps lock' to release capitals.
- Begin keying in.

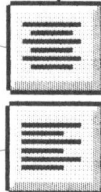

To centre a heading that has been keyed in at the LEFT MARGIN
- Place the cursor at the end of the heading and click on the **centre** button.

Instructions for tasks 1–5
- **Before** keying in the heading, follow the instructions for centring.
- Key in the paragraph.

Instructions for tasks 6–9
- **After** keying in the heading at the left margin, follow the instructions for centring.
- Key in the paragraph.
- Proof-read your work.
- Correct any errors.
- Print a copy of your work.

FOLENS IT – *Keyboard Skills Book 3*   © Folens (copiable page)

Section 2 – tasks 1 to 5

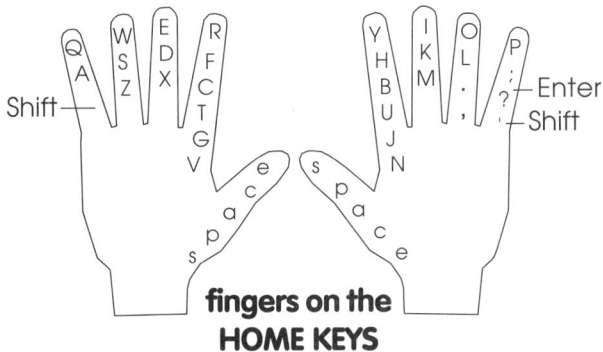

Shift

Enter
Shift

fingers on the HOME KEYS

Task 1

MONSTERS

Some of the monsters mentioned below are myths, others actually did exist. Can we be certain which are real and which are not?

Task 2

SCYLLA

This was a fantastic sea serpent that had six heads. It lived in a cave on the coast of Sicily. Its favourite diet appears to have been passing sailors.

Task 3

NANDIBEAR

This giant bear is believed to live in east Africa. It eats flesh. The people of the Nandi tribe say it wanders about after dark making blood-curdling screams. Its footprint is supposed to be four times the size of a human's.

Task 4

ROC

This was an immense bird that appeared in the legend 'Sinbad the Sailor'. It was supposed to be big enough to eat an elephant, holding it in its huge talons. The Roc was like an eagle, with a wing span of 10 metres.

Task 5

THE LAMBTON WORM

John Lambton lived in the north of England. One day when fishing in the River Wear he caught a hideous worm. To get rid of it, he threw it into a nearby well. Seven years later the worm, now very large, crept out of the well and slid back into the River Wear. Every night it came on to the land and rampaged around the countryside, killing animals and people. No one managed to kill it until John Lambton decided to ask a witch, who told him to wear clothes with sharp spikes. When he fought the worm it coiled itself around him and was cut to shreds. It fell back into the River Wear and was never seen again.

Section 2 – tasks 6 to 9

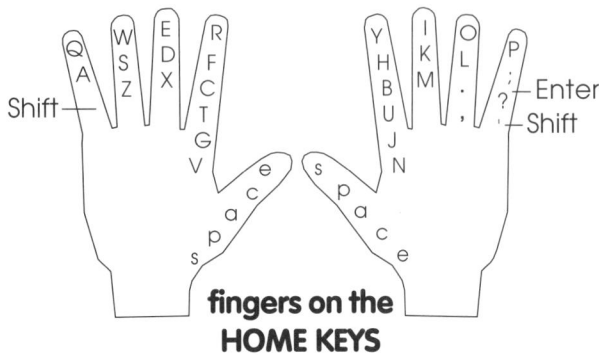

fingers on the HOME KEYS

Task 6

THE KRAKEN

Shaped like an octopus or squid, these giant sea creatures were said to have many arms that could get hold of someone and lift them from a boat. They were supposed to be strong enough to drag a boat down to the bottom of the ocean. They were once thought to be a legend, but there is now proof that giant squids exist. The old Norse word 'Kraken' means 'giant sea monster'.

Task 7

WEREWOLVES

Fact or fiction? From all over the world come tales of people who change into wolves at every full moon. Many books have been written about them and films made of them. Werewolves kill and eat human beings. The only way they can be killed is by shooting them with a silver bullet.

Task 8

THE ABOMINABLE SNOWMAN

This is a beast covered in brown shaggy hair. Another name for it is the Yeti. It is said to be about 2 metres tall, powerfully built, with long arms and a hairless face. It walks upright like a human and is supposed to be shy. There are no known photographs of the Abominable Snowman or its cousin, the Sasquatch, supposed to live in the forests of North America. The Snowman is said to live high in the Himalayas and is nocturnal. There is no real proof that either of these beasts really exists.

Task 9

THE LOCH NESS MONSTER

The most famous photograph of the Loch Ness Monster was taken in 1934 by Colonel Robert Wilson. In the picture, the head and neck of a sea serpent are visible. Loch Ness is 297 metres deep. In AD565, St. Columbo made the earliest reference to a monster in Loch Ness. He wrote in his diary about the burial of a man who was bitten to death by a water beast while he was swimming in the Loch.

Section 3
Centring complete documents

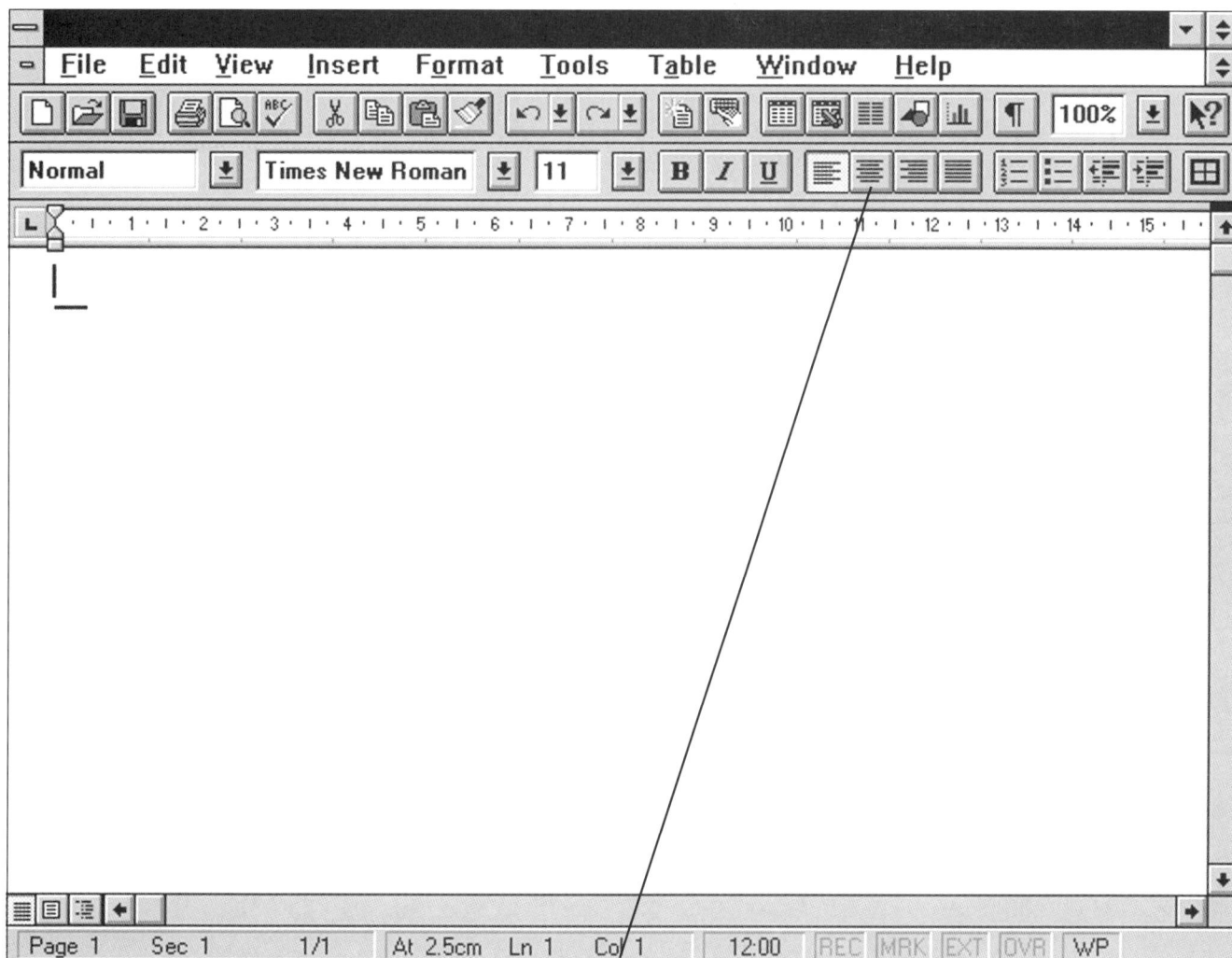

```
┌─────────────────────────────────────────────────────────────────────────┐
│ ─                                                                   ▼ │ ▲ │
│ ─   File   Edit   View   Insert   Format   Tools   Table   Window   Help  ▲│
│ ┌─┐┌─┐┌─┐ ┌─┐┌─┐┌ABC┐ ┌─┐┌─┐┌─┐┌─┐ ┌─┐┌─┐┌─┐┌─┐ ┌─┐┌─┐┌─┐┌─┐┌─┐ ┌─┐ ┌100%┐┌─┐ ┌▶?┐ │
│ Normal        ▼  Times New Roman  ▼  11   ▼   B  I  U   ≡ ≡ ≡ ≡   ≡ ≡ ≡ ≡  ⊞ │
│ L ▽ · ı · 1 · ı · 2 · ı · 3 · ı · 4 · ı · 5 · ı · 6 · ı · 7 · ı · 8 · ı · 9 · ı · 10 · ı · 11 · ı · 12 · ı · 13 · ı · 14 · ı · 15 · ı · ↑│
│ │                                                                         │
│ ‖_                                                                        │
│                                                                           │
│                                                                           │
│                                                                           │
│                                                                           │
│                                                                           │
│                                                                           │
│                                                                         ↓ │
│ ≡ ▣ ⧉ ←                                                                  → │
│ Page 1   Sec 1      1/1     At 2.5cm   Ln 1   Col 1     12:00  REC MRK EXT OVR WP │
└─────────────────────────────────────────────────────────────────────────┘
```

Instructions for Section 3

To centre a document BEFORE keying in
● Click on the **centre** button.
● Key in as normal.

To centre a document that has been keyed in at the LEFT MARGIN
● Place the mouse pointer at the top left-hand corner of the text to be centred.
● Click on the mouse and drag the pointer to the bottom right-hand corner of the text. All of the text should now be highlighted.
● Click on the centre button.

Instructions for tasks 1 and 2
● Click on the centre button.
● Key in the advertisements.

Instructions for tasks 3 and 4
● Key in the advertisements at the left margin.
● Highlight and centre the text.

Note
● In each task, press the enter/return key three times after the heading and twice between each block of text.
● Proof-read your work, correct any errors.
● Print a copy of your work.

Section 3 – tasks 1 and 2

Task 1

> FOR SALE
>
> Scylla
> A six-headed serpent
>
> Newly arrived from Sicily this century
>
> House-trained
> Requires simple diet of foreign sailors
>
> Free to a good home

Task 2

> WANTED
>
> Companion for three lonely sisters
>
> Young men with swords need not apply
> Opportunity to study ancient stone statues
>
> Would suit a hairdresser
>
> Apply in writing to MEDUSA
> Box Number 1

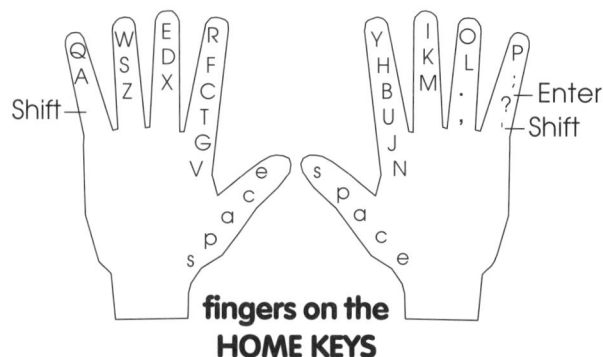

fingers on the HOME KEYS

Section 3 – tasks 3 and 4

Task 3

LESSONS IN MONSTER SLAYING

Personal lessons given by an expert from the north of England

Guaranteed success every time

Book now to avoid disappointment
Ring Lambton Castle for details

Cheap rates for OAPs

Task 4

LOST

Old lady, plump, white hair
Dressed in tartan skirt

Last seen in the Loch Ness area with a periscope
May have hired a boat for fishing trip

Please contact:
Freedom for Grannies Group, London

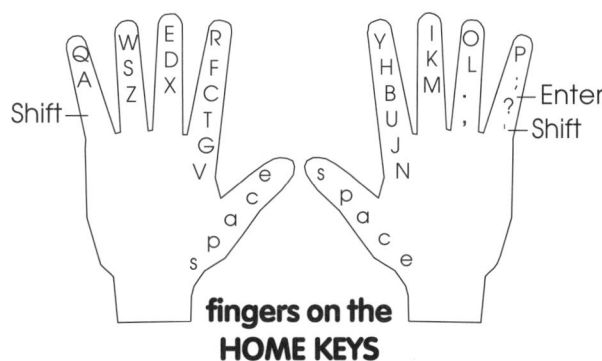

fingers on the
HOME KEYS

Section 4
Changing paragraphs and text

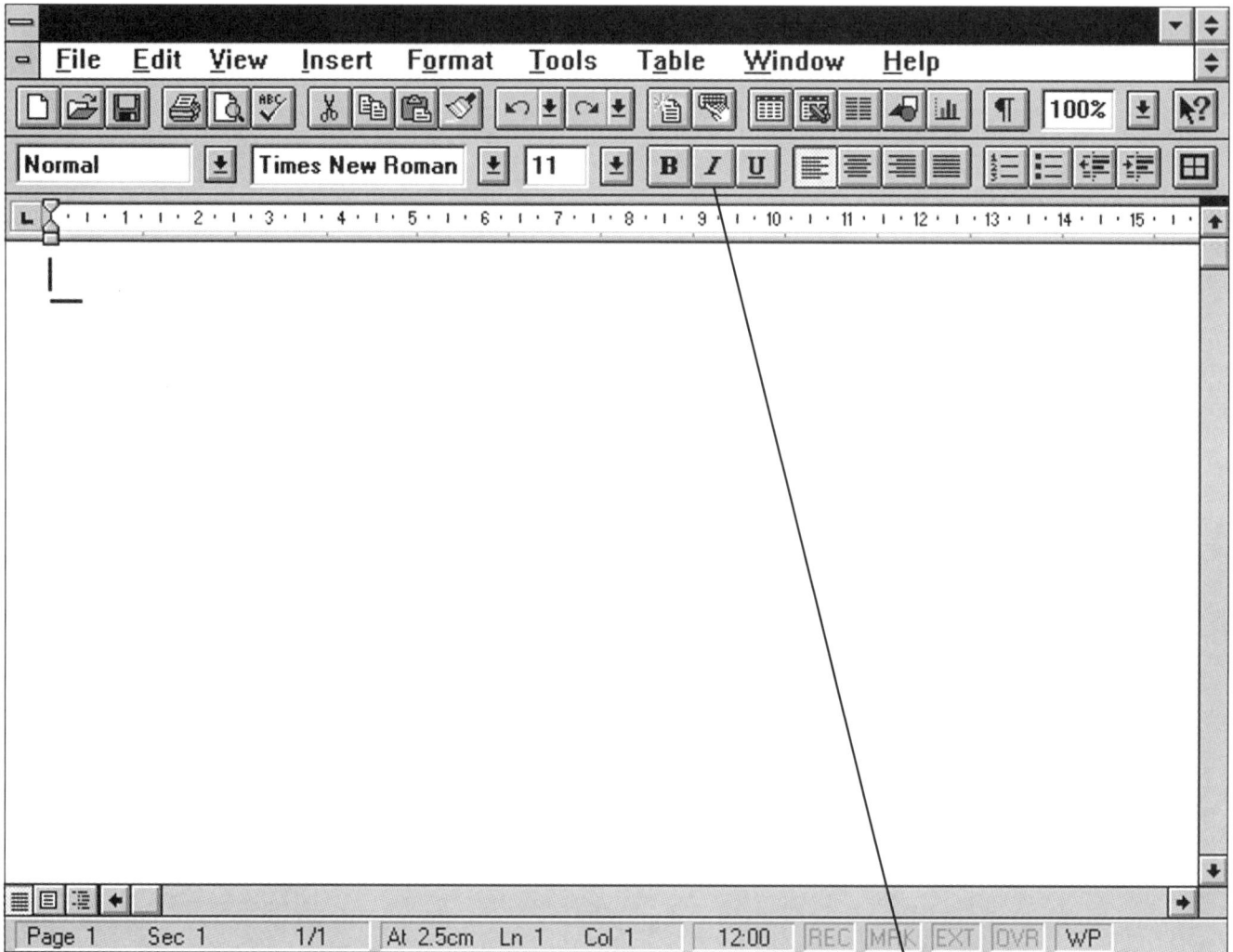

File   Edit   View   Insert   Format   Tools   Table   Window   Help

Normal   Times New Roman   11   **B** *I* U

| 1 · 1 · 2 · 1 · 3 · 1 · 4 · 1 · 5 · 1 · 6 · 1 · 7 · 1 · 8 · 1 · 9 · 1 · 10 · 1 · 11 · 1 · 12 · 1 · 13 · 1 · 14 · 1 · 15 · 1 · |

Page 1   Sec 1   1/1   At 2.5cm   Ln 1   Col 1   12:00   REC   MRK   EXT   OVR   WP

B *I* U

Instructions for Section 4

To join paragraphs
- Place the cursor at the beginning of the lower paragraph to be joined.
- Press the delete/backspace key twice.
- Adjust the spacing if necessary.

To split paragraphs
- Place the cursor at the beginning of the sentence that will start the new paragraph.
- Press the enter/return key twice.
- Adjust the spacing if necessary.

To change text to bold, italic or underline
- To change text **before** keying in, click on the button you need, key in the words, then click on the same button again.
- To change text **after** keying in, highlight the text using the mouse, then click on the button you need.

Instructions for tasks 1–5
- Key in the text.
- Make the changes.
- Proof-read your work, correct any errors.
- Print a copy of your work.

Section 4 – task 1

GHOSTS AND GHOULS

What are ghosts? Are they just part of the imagination, or do they really exist? The first ghost story was written on a clay tablet in the year 2,000BC. Ever since then, ghost stories have been told all over the world.

Evil spirits, poltergeists, werewolves and vampires are big business in the film world. Horror films and even comedy films are sometimes made about ghosts and hauntings.

Watching ghost stories in a cinema or on the television can be scary, but it is when you are alone in the dark that strange creaks and groans can become really frightening. When dark shadows are everywhere and you can hear the howl of the wind – this is when the imagination takes over and the real terror begins.

In the past, people believed in ghosts when their houses were lit by candles or the strange gleam from gas lights. However, now we can easily get rid of our fears by simply switching on the light!

Changes

1. Centre the heading, underline it and make it bold.

2. In the first paragraph, make bold the first sentence.

3. In the second paragraph, make italic the first sentence.

4. In the third paragraph, make a new paragraph beginning 'When dark shadows'.

5. Join the first two paragraphs to make a single paragraph.

6. Join the last two paragraphs to make a single paragraph.

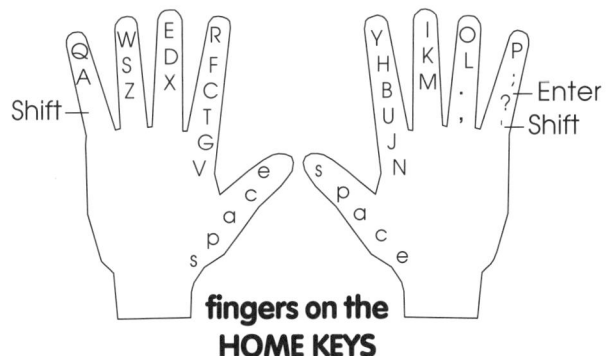

fingers on the
HOME KEYS

Section 4 – task 2

DREAMS

We don't always remember our dreams, even though we dream whenever we are asleep. The dreams we do remember are those we have as we are falling asleep, or waking up. These dreams are sometimes so faint that we remember them for only a few moments when we wake up.

However, there are dreams that are so vivid that they stay with us, not just all day, but sometimes for years after. Some people believe that dreams are a way of telling the future. It is also believed that dreams go in opposites, so that when we are dreaming about happiness, it could really mean that we are dreaming about sorrow.

These ideas about dreams have been around for a long time. The Ancient Greeks and Romans were the first people to write about dreams in 'dream books'. They believed that dreams were messages from the gods. Even today, many books are written about dreams and what they could mean.

Changes

1. Centre the heading, underline it and make it bold.

2. Make italic the word 'dreams' throughout the text.

3. In the third paragraph, underline the words 'Ancient Greeks and Romans'.

4. In the third paragraph, make bold the words 'Even today'.

5. In the second paragraph, make a new paragraph beginning 'It is also believed that'.

6. Join the last two paragraphs to make a single paragraph.

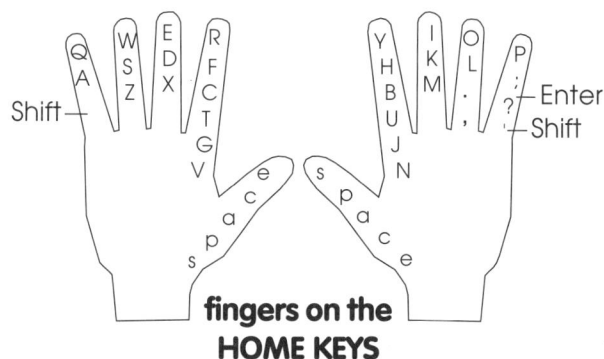

fingers on the HOME KEYS

FOLENS IT – *Keyboard Skills Book 3*   © Folens (copiable page)

Section 4 – task 3

PHANTOMS

Stories of ghosts that look like human beings are quite common. However, many people do not know that there are also stories of phantom aeroplanes, buses, cars and even dogs.

There is a well-known story of a phantom dog called 'Black Shuck'. It stood as tall as a calf and had one red eye, the size of a saucer, in the middle of its forehead. If that wasn't enough, this phantom dog went around howling, with fire and foam coming from its jaws. Death or disaster struck anyone who saw 'Black Shuck'.

There are also stories of phantom aeroplanes. Biggin Hill is an airfield that was used during the Second World War. It is said to be haunted by a phantom Spitfire fighter plane. Perhaps the plane was shot down and the pilot was killed, but the ghostly engines of his aeroplane have been heard for miles around.

Changes

1. Centre the heading, underline it and make it bold.

2. In the second paragraph, make italic the words 'Black Shuck'.

3. In the third paragraph, underline the words 'Biggin Hill'.

4. In the third paragraph, make bold the word 'Spitfire'.

5. In the second paragraph, make a new paragraph beginning 'If that wasn't enough'.

6. Join the first two paragraphs to make a single paragraph.

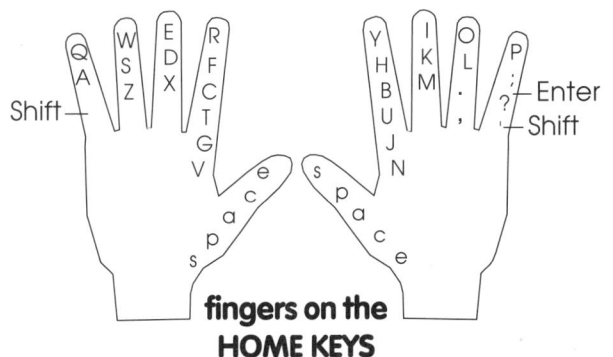

fingers on the
HOME KEYS

Section 4 – task 4

BLACK HOLES

What is a 'black hole'? How do astronomers know they exist if they can't see them? Of all the strange objects in the universe, black holes must be the most fascinating. There have been many books and stories about adventures in space and exploring black holes, but in reality very little is known about them.

After a star has blown up, in what is called a 'supernova' explosion, the centre of the star collapses until it is only a tiny pin-point in space. It is, however, surrounded by a more powerful force of gravity than a normal star. When the astronomers detect this powerful force of gravity, even though the star itself is too far away to be seen, they know that a black hole exists there.

To get out of a black hole is impossible. To do so you would have to travel at a speed faster than light, but nothing can travel faster than that. This is why these strange objects have been called 'black holes' – not even light can escape from them.

Changes

1. Centre the heading, underline it and make it bold.

2. Make bold the words 'black hole' and 'black holes' throughout the text.

3. Make italic the words 'astronomers' throughout the text.

4. In the third paragraph, underline the words 'faster than light'.

5. In the second paragraph, make a new paragraph beginning 'When the'.

6. Join the last two paragraphs to make a single paragraph.

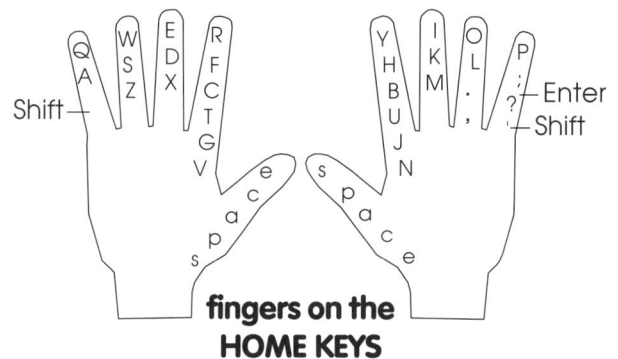

fingers on the HOME KEYS

Section 4 – task 5

THE RING OF FIRE

The Ring of Fire is the name given to the shoreline around the great Pacific Ocean. It is so called because this is where many of the world's most active volcanoes are.

The Pacific Ocean is nearly ten times as big as the largest country in the world – Russia. The average depth of this huge ocean is 4,282 metres, but at a certain point, called the Marianas Trench, the ocean floor drops to a depth of 11,033 metres. This is the deepest point on Earth.

The Hawaiian Islands are in the Pacific Ocean and one of Hawaii's volcanic mountains, Mount Kea, is really the highest mountain in the world. This mountain is said to measure 10,203 metres from its base, which is on the ocean floor, to its top which forms an island.

In the warm waters of the South Pacific, coral reefs grow in the shallows around the coastline of the islands. Coral reefs are grown by tiny animals whose skeletons are outside their bodies.

Changes

1. Centre the heading, underline it and make it bold.

2. In the first paragraph, make italic the words 'Ring of Fire'.

3. In the second paragraph, make bold the words 'Marianas Trench'.

4. In the third paragraph, underline the words 'Mount Kea'.

5. Join the first two paragraphs to make a single paragraph.

6. In the last paragraph, make a new paragraph beginning 'Coral reefs are'.

fingers on the
HOME KEYS

Section 5
Indenting the first line and making columns

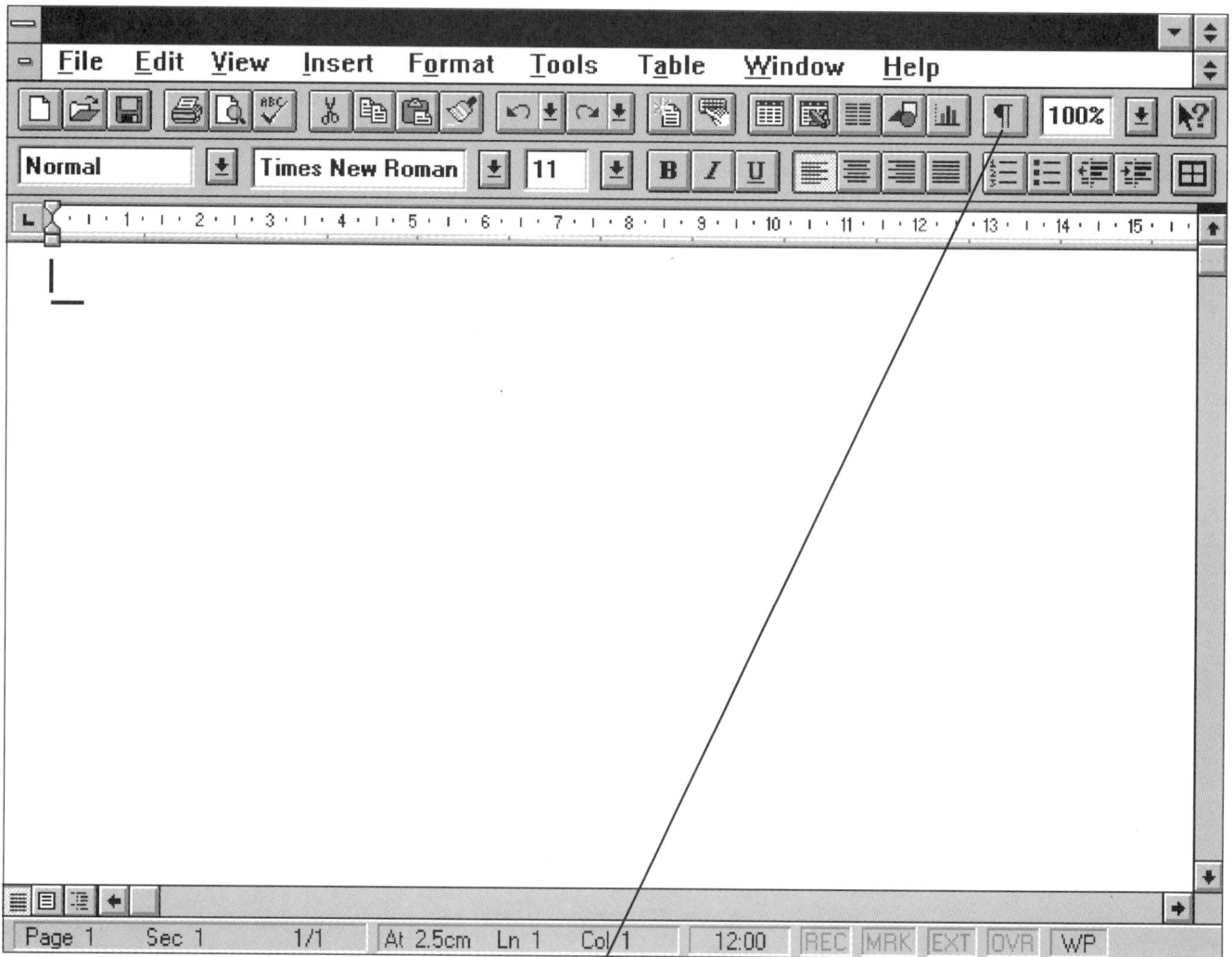

Instructions for Section 5

Use the symbols
- Click on the show/hide button
  to show symbols on the screen.

To indent the first line of a paragraph
- Press the tab key once ➡.

To make two columns
- Press the tab key twice ➡ ➡.
- Key in the first line of the first column.
- Press the tab key twice again ➡ ➡.
- Key in the first line of the second column.
  Press enter/return.
- Continue, keeping the columns in line.

Instructions for tasks 1–3
- Centre the heading and make it bold,
  then press enter/return twice.
- **Note:** the first line of the first paragraph
  should not be indented.
- Indent the first line of all the other
  paragraphs.
- Key in the columns.
- Proof-read your work, correct any errors.
- Print a copy of your work.

Section 5 – task 1

VOLCANOES

One of the most famous volcanoes was Mount Vesuvius in Italy. In AD79 Mount Vesuvius erupted and buried the town of Pompeii, killing all the people who lived there.

➡ Another famous eruption was in 1883 when Krakatoa, which is a group of volcanic cones, became active. Two of the cones exploded and a third split in two. The blasts from this shattering explosion were heard nearly 5,000 kilometres away in India, China and Australia. Volcanic ash was thrown many kilometres into the air. The dust was so thick that it was dark for two days.

➡ As a result of this explosion a huge tidal wave was formed. This was said to have reached a height of 39 metres. The wave crashed down on the islands of Java and Sumatra, killing over 36,000 people.

➡ These are some of the world's volcanoes and the date they last erupted:
- ➡ ➡ Vesuvius – AD79
- ➡ ➡ Taupo – AD150
- ➡ ➡ Tambora – 1815
- ➡ ➡ Krakatoa – 1883
- ➡ ➡ Mont Pelee – 1902
- ➡ ➡ Katmai – 1912
- ➡ ➡ Mount Etna – 1974
- ➡ ➡ Mount St. Helens – 1980
- ➡ ➡ Pinatubo – 1991
- ➡ ➡ Mauna Loa – still active

➡ A great many myths and legends surrounded volcanic activity many years ago. Some primitive people believed that a huge whale lived inside the volcano. Others believed that a great spider lived there. Apparently, the Indonesians believed that a giant snake, by the name of Hontobogo, lived in their volcano and held up the whole world. They believed that when the snake got angry and started to move, the whole world shook.

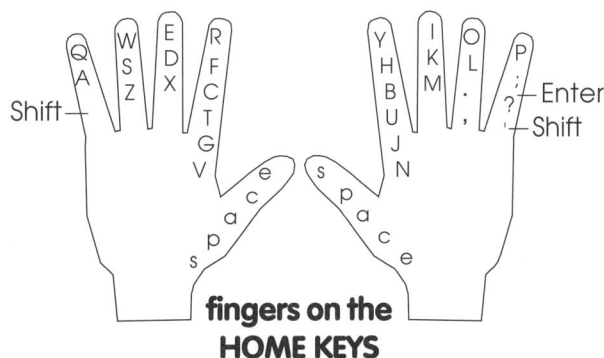

Shift

Enter
Shift

fingers on the HOME KEYS

Section 5 – task 2

FORTUNE-TELLING

The art of fortune-telling using cards came many centuries ago from the East. The first pack of cards was made in Europe, for the mad King of France, Charles VI, in 1392.

➡ The first cards had acorns, leaves, hearts and bells on them, instead of the hearts, diamonds, clubs and spades that we know so well today.

➡ If you ever decide to have your fortune told, it is said that Monday and Friday are especially good days. However, for the best results, it seems that the early evening is the best time to consult the cards.

➡ The fortune-teller usually chooses a card to go with each customer. People with grey or white hair are counted as fair haired.

➡ ➡ A young fair man or woman ➡ ➡ The King or Queen of Hearts
➡ ➡ A dark young man or woman ➡ ➡ The King or Queen of Clubs
➡ ➡ A dark elderly man or woman ➡ ➡ The King or Queen of Spades
➡ ➡ An elderly fair man or woman ➡ ➡ The King or Queen of Diamonds

➡ The four suits have the following meaning when they are read as part of your fortune:

➡ ➡ Clubs ➡ ➡ Power, fame, ability and money
➡ ➡ Spades ➡ ➡ Misfortune, suffering, loss and treachery
➡ ➡ Hearts ➡ ➡ Love, affection, friendship and sympathy
➡ ➡ Diamonds ➡ ➡ Travel, voyages, business and adventure

➡ A word of warning! The predictions from fortune-telling with cards are only quite simple ideas of the direction in which your life could go!

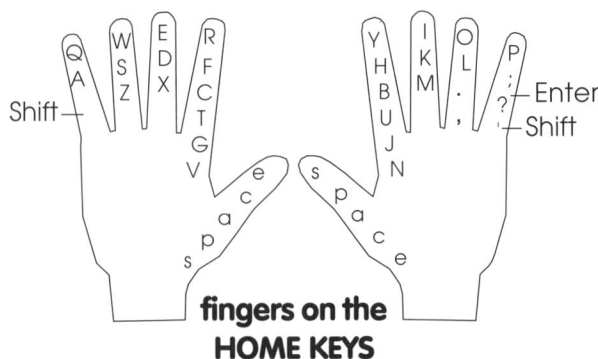

fingers on the
HOME KEYS

Section 5 – task 3

DID I SEE A GHOST?

How would you know if you had seen a ghost? Research shows that ghosts appear in many different ways.

➡ For instance, some ghosts are said to be transparent, misty shapes that shimmer and sway from side to side. Others are said to be more solid, dark, shadowy figures. Then there is the lifelike figure that suddenly appears and just as suddenly disappears.

➡ Fortunately, ghosts tend to behave in similar ways. Listed below are a few of the things they have in common.

➡ ➡ Ghosts almost never speak   ➡ ➡ They vanish quickly
➡ ➡ Hover above the ground   ➡ ➡ Wear old-fashioned clothes
➡ ➡ Disappear through a wall   ➡ ➡ Appear suddenly from nowhere
➡ ➡ Often appear at night   ➡ ➡ Sometimes look unhappy

➡ Unless you are what is called psychic, it is unlikely that you will ever be lucky (or unlucky) enough to see a ghost. Research shows that sometimes the temperature drops suddenly, just before a ghost appears. A sudden cold chill that makes the hairs on your arms stand up, or makes you shiver, could mean that something is about to appear.

➡ However, sightings of ghosts still seem to be very rare. Many people simply refuse to believe that ghosts exist! These people say that there are ways of explaining ghosts.

➡ ➡ Day-dreaming   ➡ ➡ Being tired
➡ ➡ Imagination   ➡ ➡ Being scared of the dark
➡ ➡ Wind in the trees   ➡ ➡ Someone playing a practical joke!

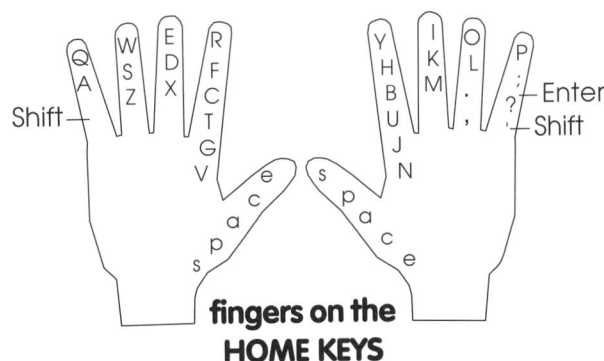

fingers on the
HOME KEYS

Section 6
Copying blocks of text

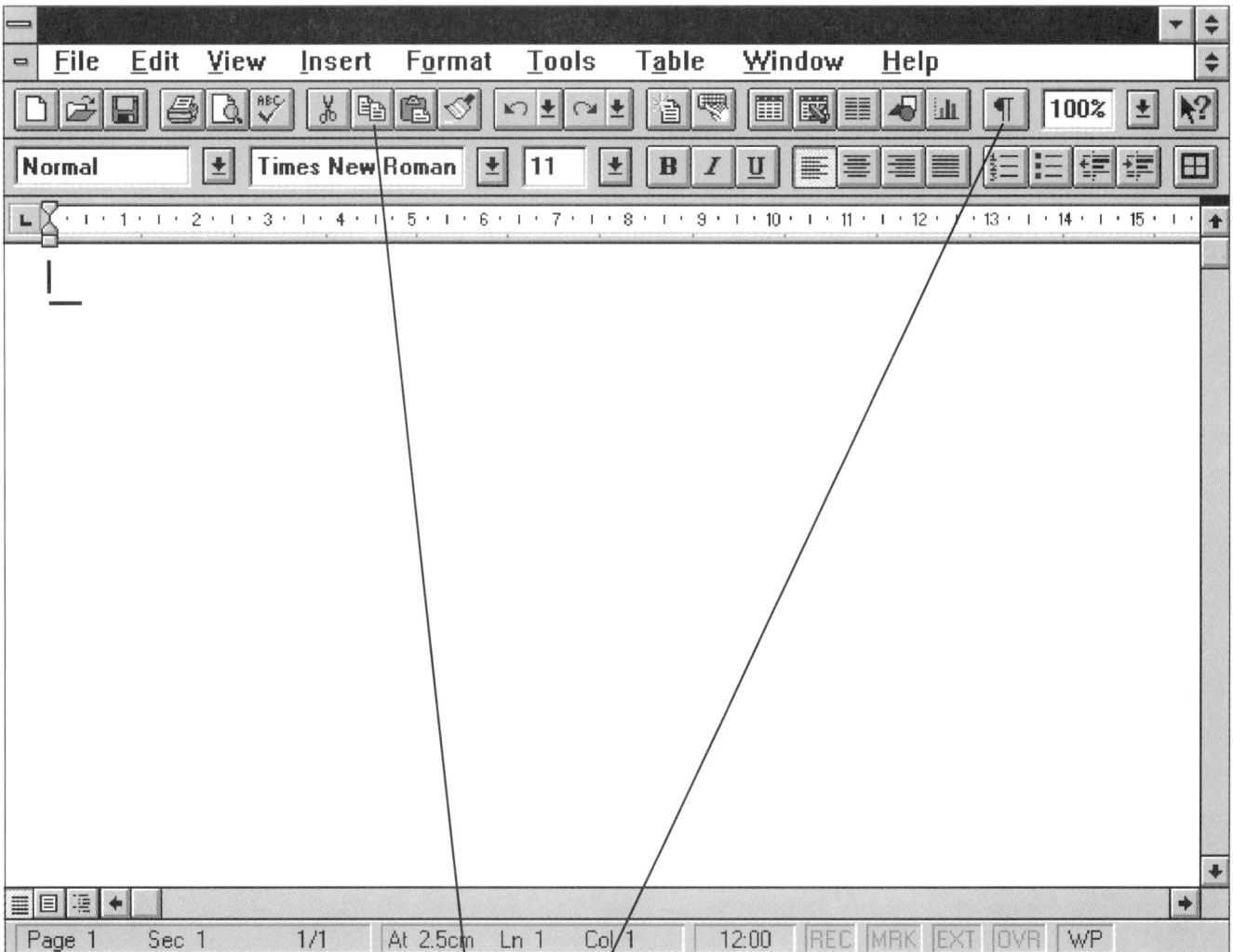

Instructions for Section 6

Use the symbols
- Click on the show/hide button to show symbols on the screen.

To copy a block of text
- Key in the text.
- Press the enter/return key twice.
- Highlight the text.
- Click on the copy button.
- Move the mouse pointer to the lower ¶ paragraph mark.
- Click on the paste button. A copy of the text appears.

Instructions for tasks 1–3
- Make the heading bold.
- Key in the text.
- Highlight the text and copy it.
- Make two copies of each notice.
- Proof-read your work, correct any errors.
- Print a copy of your work.

FOLENS IT – *Keyboard Skills Book 3*   © Folens (copiable page)

Section 6 – tasks 1 to 3

Task 1

GHOST BUSTERS

Fully equipped team of highly qualified, professional Ghost Busters. Have expertise and will travel.

All kinds of ghosts and phantoms can be investigated. Fees negotiable. Contact Spectre 356234.

GHOST BUSTERS

Fully equipped team of highly qualified, professional Ghost Busters. Have expertise and will travel.

All kinds of ghosts and phantoms can be investigated. Fees negotiable. Contact Spectre 356234.

Task 2

WANTED

Ghost-hunting equipment. Need hearing aid and infra-red camera. Must be in good condition. Required urgently for desperate occupants of a haunted house. Reply to Mr Jones, Rose Court.

WANTED

Ghost-hunting equipment. Need hearing aid and infra-red camera. Must be in good condition. Required urgently for desperate occupants of a haunted house. Reply to Mr Jones, Rose Court.

Task 3

PHANTOMS ANONYMOUS

A meeting will be held on Friday 13th. All phantoms and ghosts welcome.

A talk will be given by the Guardian of the Graveyard on 'How to contact the living'. Walls open at 13 o'clock. Admission free.

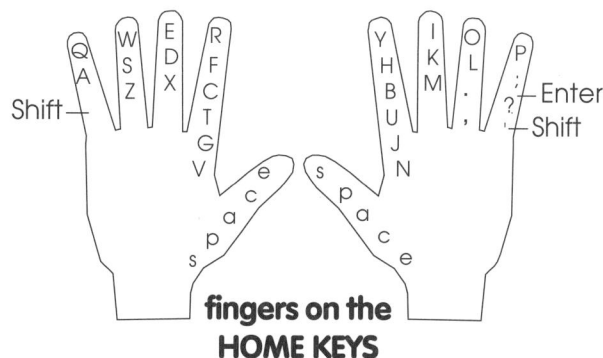

PHANTOMS ANONYMOUS

A meeting will be held on Friday 13th. All phantoms and ghosts welcome.

A talk will be given by the Guardian of the Graveyard on 'How to contact the living'. Walls open at 13 o'clock. Admission free.

fingers on the HOME KEYS

Section 7
Moving and justifying text

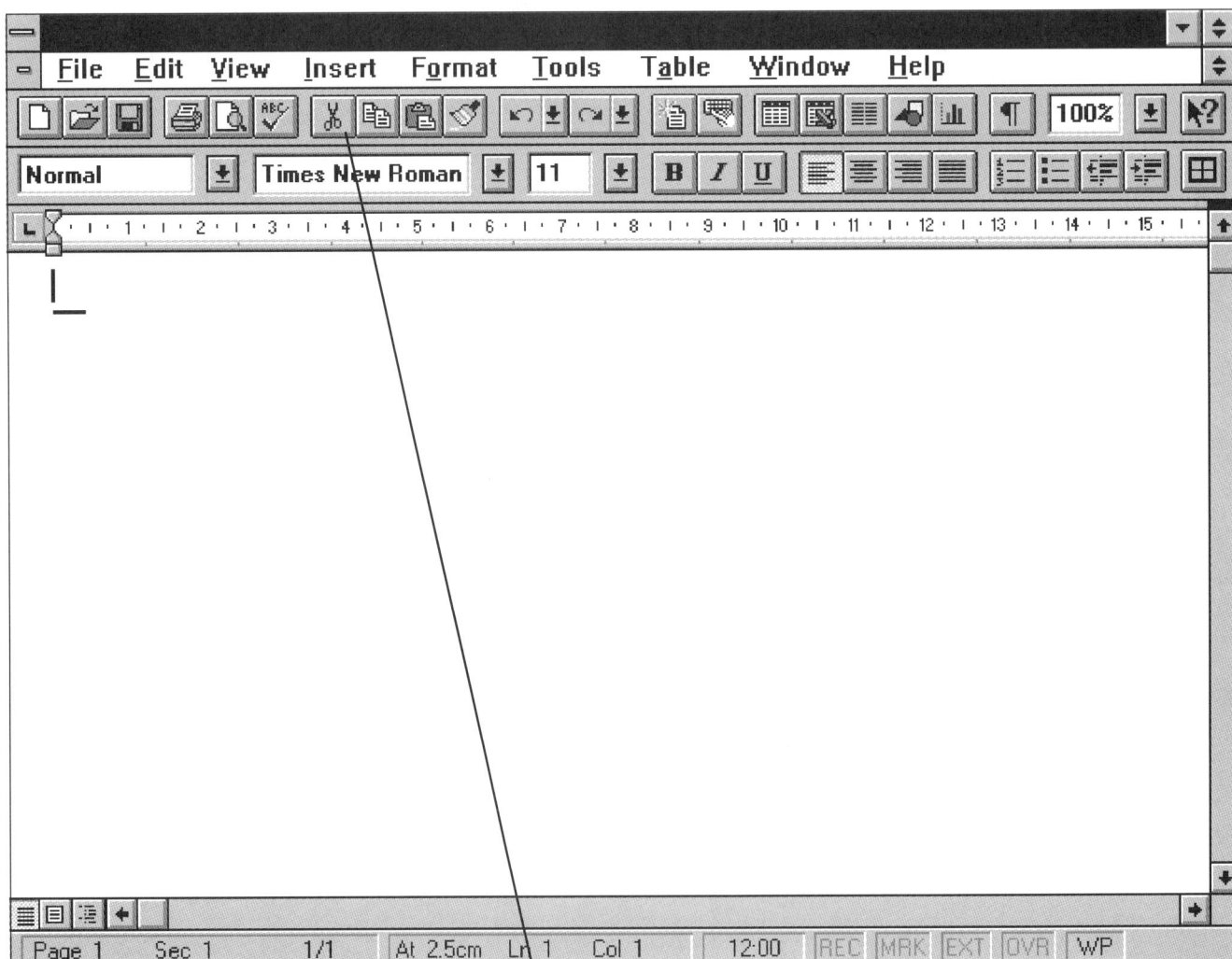

```
┌────────────────────────────────────────────────────────────────────────┐
│ ─                                                                  ▼  ▲▼ │
│ ─  File  Edit  View  Insert  Format  Tools  Table  Window  Help        ▲▼│
│ [□][☞][▤] [⎙][▨][ᵃᵇᶜ] [✄][▤][▤][◈] [↶][↧][↷][↧] [▨][▨] [▦][▦][▤][▨][ⅈⅈ] [¶] [100%][±] [▸²]│
│ [Normal    ][±] [Times New Roman][±][11][±] [B][I][U] [▤][▤][▤][▤] [▤][▤][▤][▤][⊞]│
│ L ▯ ·ı·1·ı·2·ı·3·ı·4·ı·5·ı·6·ı·7·ı·8·ı·9·ı·10·ı·11·ı·12·ı·13·ı·14·ı·15·ı· ▲│
│   │                                                                       │
│   │ I                                                                     │
│   │ ─                                                                     │
│   │                                                                       │
│   │                                                                       │
│   │                                                                     ▼ │
│ [▤][▤][▤][←]                                                          [→]│
│ │Page 1   Sec 1      1/1   │At 2.5cm  Ln 1   Col 1  │  12:00  │REC│MRK│EXT│OVR│WP││
└────────────────────────────────────────────────────────────────────────┘
```

Instructions for Section 7

To move a block of text
- Highlight the text.
- Click on the cut button.
- Move the mouse pointer and click where you want the text.
- Click on the paste button.

To justify text
- To justify text **before** keying in, click on the justify button, then key in the text.
- To justify text **after** keying in, highlight the text, then click on the justify button.

To delete a block of text
- Highlight the text to be deleted.
- Click on the cut button.
- Adjust spacing if necessary.

Instructions for tasks 1–3
- Before task 1, click on the justify button. Before tasks 2 and 3, click on the left button.
- Make the changes.
- Proof-read your work, correct any errors.
- Print a copy of your work.

FOLENS IT – *Keyboard Skills Book 3*

Section 7 – task 1

TOO MANY PEOPLE

There were 5,500 million people in the world in 1992 and it is estimated that by the year 2000 there will be over 6,000 million. The population grows every day by almost 250,000 people.

If we all held hands we could make a chain that would go around the world 90 times! However, if everyone in the world stood shoulder to shoulder we could fit into an area the size of the Island of Anglesey.

One person in five lives in China, which has a population of about 1,160 million. India's population is growing so fast that it is estimated that by the year 2050 it will have reached 1,600 million.

The least populated country in the world is Mongolia. Only 2 million people live there, although it is six times bigger than Great Britain.

It is only since 1950 that the world's population has grown so quickly. Apparently, 10,000 years ago there were only about 5 million people in the whole world – less than there is today in London.

Changes

1. In the first paragraph, delete the last sentence starting 'The population grows'.

2. Move the last paragraph so that it becomes the second paragraph.

3. Move the fourth paragraph so that it becomes the fifth paragraph.

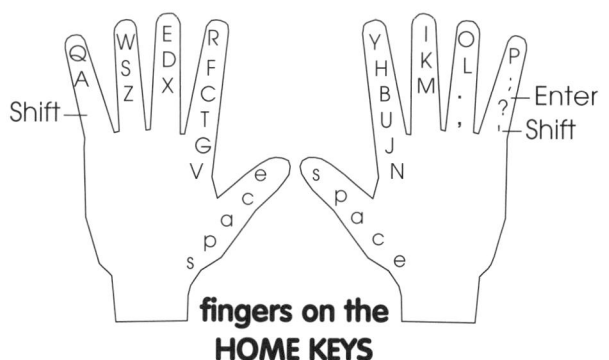

fingers on the
HOME KEYS

Section 7 – task 2

GREEN GIANTS

Of all living things, trees can grow higher, weigh heavier and live longer than any other plant or animal.

'General Sherman' is a giant sequoia tree and is the most massive living thing of all time. It is 13 times heavier than the largest animal, the Blue Whale. General Sherman weighs about 2,500 tonnes and is estimated to be around 3,000 years old. Its trunk is said to measure 25 metres at its widest point.

Growing high in the Rocky Mountains of Nevada is the bristlecone pine. It is said to be the world's oldest living tree, estimated to be more than an incredible 5,000 years old!

The ginko tree is called a 'fossil tree' because it is said to have leaves that are almost exactly the same as fossilised leaves that have been preserved in rock. There were ginko trees living millions of years ago, at the same time as the dinosaurs, so they are probably the oldest variety of tree alive today.

Changes

1. Move the second paragraph so that it becomes the first paragraph.

2. Move the third paragraph beginning 'Growing high' so that it becomes the last paragraph.

3. In the paragraph beginning 'The ginko tree', delete the last sentence.

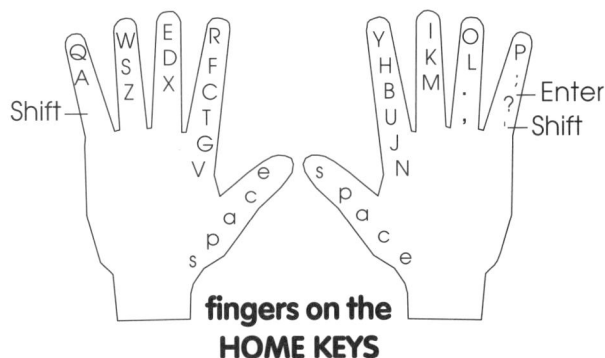

fingers on the
HOME KEYS

FOLENS IT – *Keyboard Skills Book 3*   © Folens (copiable page)

Section 7 – task 3

EARTHQUAKES

Earthquakes often happen in those parts of the world where volcanoes occur. During an earthquake, there is a noise like the roar of an express train. Buildings crack and collapse, the ground heaves and great cracks appear. These are some of the very frightening effects of an earthquake.

The surface of the Earth is made up of 'plates' that are moving all the time. An earthquake occurs when pressure builds up between two plates. One of the most severe earthquakes ever recorded was in Anchorage, Alaska, in 1964.

Fortunately the area where the earthquake occurred was remote and the number of people killed was low. A huge wave said to be the highest ever recorded, 67 metres high, followed the Alaskan earthquake.

Thousands of people have been killed in other earthquakes because they occurred in heavily populated areas. In 1976 the Tang-Shan earthquake in eastern China is thought to have killed 655,000 people. A full report of the tragedy was never released by the Chinese government, so the real extent of the earthquake will never be known.

Changes

1. Move the first paragraph so that it becomes the last paragraph.

2. In the paragraph beginning 'Thousands of people have', delete the last sentence.

3. Justify the whole passage.

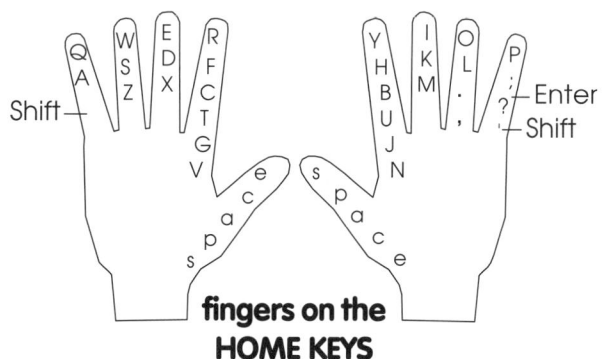

fingers on the
HOME KEYS

Section 8
Changing the line space and text size

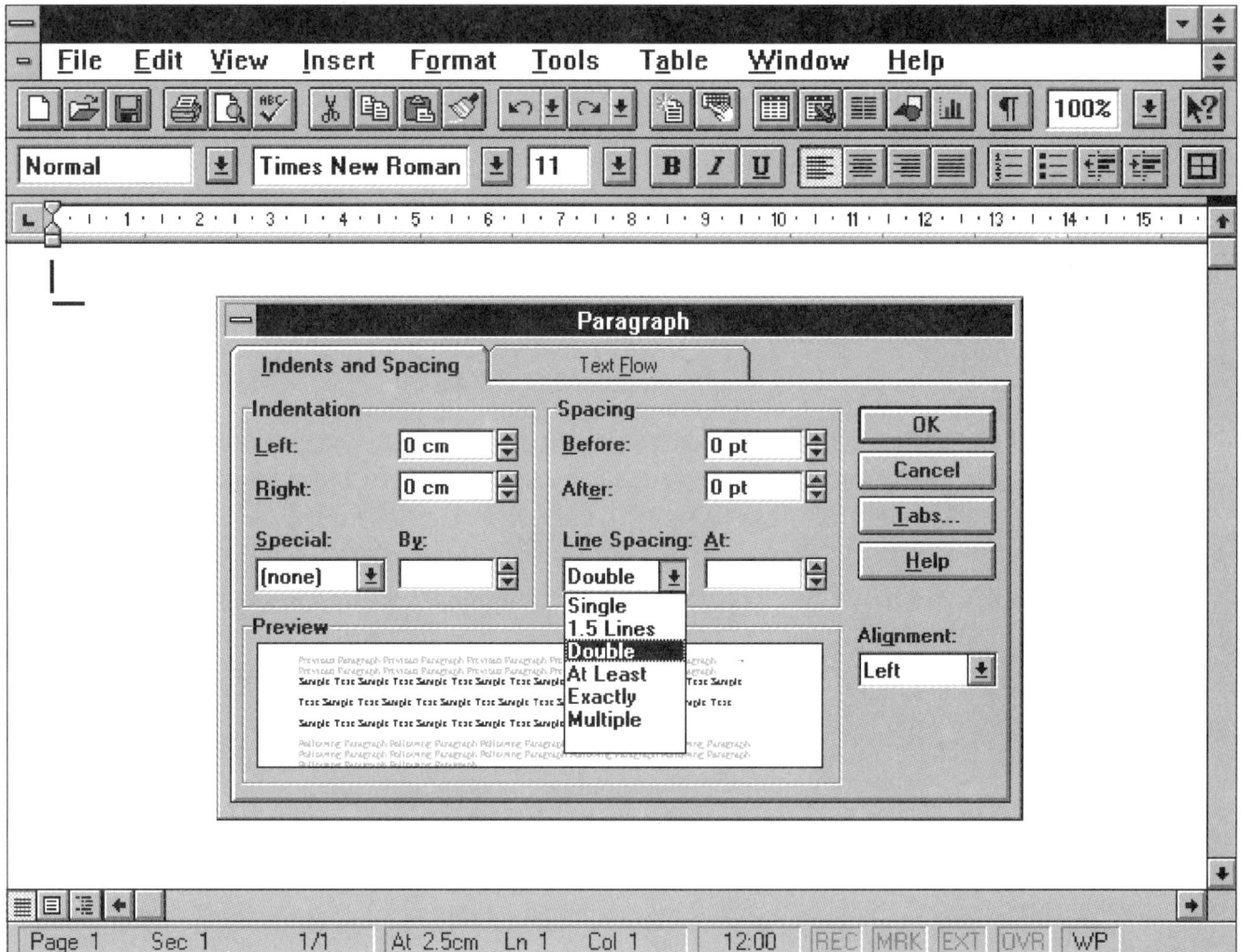

File Edit View Insert Format Tools Table Window Help

`Normal` `Times New Roman` `11` **B** *I* U

| 1 · 2 · 3 · 4 · 5 · 6 · 7 · 8 · 9 · 10 · 11 · 12 · 13 · 14 · 15 |

Paragraph

| Indents and Spacing | Text Flow |

Indentation
Left: `0 cm`
Right: `0 cm`
Special: By:
`(none)`

Spacing
Before: `0 pt`
After: `0 pt`
Line Spacing: At:
`Double`

- Single
- 1.5 Lines
- **Double**
- At Least
- Exactly
- Multiple

OK
Cancel
Tabs...
Help

Preview

Previous Paragraph Previous Paragraph Previous Paragraph Previous Paragraph Previous Paragraph Previous Paragraph Previous Paragraph Previous Paragraph Previous Paragraph
Sample Text Sample Text Sample Text Sample Text Sample Text Sample Text Sample Text Sample Text Sample Text Sample Text
Sample Text Sample Text Sample Text Sample Text Sample Text Sample Text
Following Paragraph Following Paragraph Following Paragraph Following Paragraph Following Paragraph Following Paragraph Following Paragraph Following Paragraph Following Paragraph

Alignment:
`Left`

Page 1   Sec 1   1/1   At 2.5cm   Ln 1   Col 1   12:00   REC MRK EXT OVR WP

Instructions for Section 8

To change the line space
- Click on **Format** in the menu bar.
- Click on **Paragraph**. The Paragraph box will appear.
- Click on **Indents and Spacing** at the top of the box, then click on the arrow below **Line Spacing**.
- Click on **Double**, then click on **OK**.
- To change the line space after keying in, highlight the text and follow the steps above.

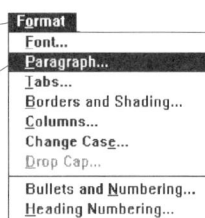

Format
Font...
Paragraph...
Tabs...
Borders and Shading...
Columns...
Change Case...
Drop Cap...
Bullets and Numbering...
Heading Numbering...

To change the size of text
- Click on the arrow next to the text size box. A list will appear.
- Click on the number you want.
- To change the size of text **after** keying in, highlight the text and follow the steps above.

14
9
10
11
12
14
16
18
20

Instructions for tasks 1–3
- Key in the task and make the changes.
- Proof-read your work, correct any errors.
- Print a copy of your work.

Section 8 – task 1

SIGHTINGS OF UFOs

There have been stories of Unidentified Flying Objects for hundreds of years. At first, these stories were kept in monasteries, because monks were the only people who could write properly.

In 1254 a sighting was recorded of a strange coloured ship that appeared in the sky over the monastery at St. Albans in Hertfordshire. In 1290 monks at Bylands Abbey in Yorkshire wrote about a sighting of a large silver disc that flew over the monastery.

There are not many more records of UFO sightings until newspapers became popular in the 1700s. In 1741 in London, Lord Beauchamp reported seeing an oval ball of fire falling from the sky. At a height of 800 metres it levelled off and disappeared with 'a long fiery tail trailing smoke'.

In 1820 at Embrun, France, a formation of saucer-shaped objects flew over the town. Keeping in formation, they turned and disappeared.

In 1833 at Niagara in the USA there was a report of 'a large square luminous object' which hovered above Niagara Falls for more than an hour before it disappeared into the distance.

Changes

1. Change the heading to 16 point size.

2. Change the first paragraph to double line spacing.

3. Change the second paragraph to 1.5 line spacing.

4. Change the last paragraph to double line spacing.

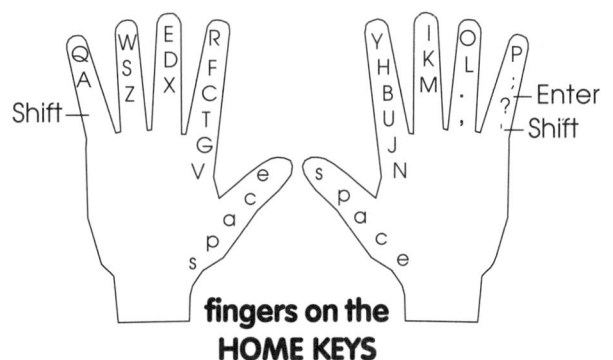

fingers on the HOME KEYS

Section 8 – task 2

THE MARTIANS ARE COMING

According to the experts, sightings of UFOs around the world often happen at certain times. One of these times was in 1952, when there were about 1,500 sightings of UFOs that year. Many of these sightings have never been properly explained.

The beginning of the spring and the summer are supposed to be the main times of the year when the largest number of UFO sightings are reported. Some people have suggested that for a certain amount of time the sightings are concentrated in one area.

An astronomer and UFO expert called Allen Hynek has put UFO sightings under three different headings. These are:

First sighting   UFO is seen in the sky or on the ground.
Second sighting   Evidence is left behind, such as a hole.
Third sighting   Creatures are seen.

Over the past 50 years there have been hundreds of reports of all three kinds of UFO sightings. Many films and television programmes have been made about UFOs and aliens, such as 'Star Trek'.

Changes

1. Change the heading to 16 point size.

2. Change all of the text to 14 point size.

3. Change all of the text to double line spacing.

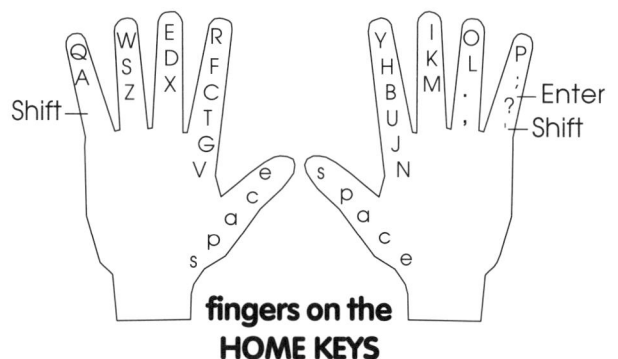

fingers on the HOME KEYS

Section 8 – task 3

GIANTS OF THE DEEP

There are many different types of whale. Scientists have been interested in these giants of the deep for many years. In fact, some scientists believe that whales could be almost as intelligent as human beings! The whale family includes Blue Whales, Sperm Whales and Whale Sharks. All whales have a thick layer of blubber that helps to keep body heat and also acts as a way of storing energy.

Although the Blue Whale is probably the largest creature on Earth, the Sperm Whale is said to be the biggest whale that has teeth. The Sperm Whale can grow to a length of 21 metres and can weigh 70 tonnes. It also has the largest brain of any animal and is capable of diving deeper than any other creature. It can dive to a depth of 3,000 metres.

The Blue Whale is much bigger than the Sperm Whale. It can grow to a length of 32 metres and weigh as much as 190 tonnes! It has no teeth. Instead it has a whalebone 'comb' that hangs down inside its mouth and traps the tiny krill (shrimps) that it lives on. It eats about 4 tonnes of krill every day.

It seems that there is not a lot known about the Whale Shark, as it is rarely seen, but it is known to weigh about 17 tonnes and measure up to 15 metres long. It has a huge mouth and can easily get two divers inside at the same time!

Changes

1. Change the heading to 14 point size.

2. Change the first paragraph to 12 point size.

3. Change the third paragraph to 11 point size.

4. Change all of the text to 1.5 line spacing.

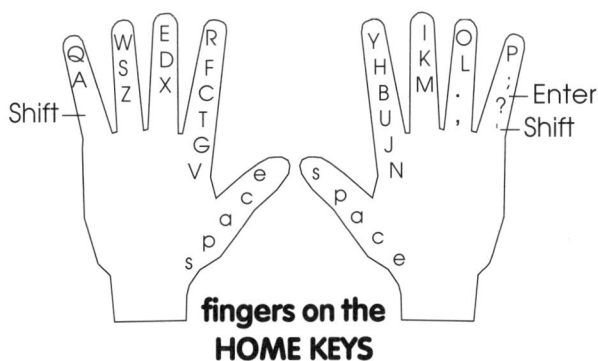

fingers on the
HOME KEYS

Section 9
Formal letter writing

	16 Park View
press enter twice	Northend
	Westshire
	NO6 8RD

23rd April 1999

Mrs J Brown
Manager
Graphics Galore Limited
3 West Way
Newtown
Westshire
NO8 9WY

press enter twice

Dear Mrs Brown

I am writing to complain about
....
....

I purchased the goods at .... and the ....
....
....
....

press enter twice

Please reply as soon as possible with ....
....
....

I look forward to hearing from you shortly.

Yours sincerely

(signature)

press enter five times

(your name)

Instructions for Section 9

Structuring your letter

- The first paragraph should say why the letter is being written.
- The middle paragraphs should give all the details you need to include.
- The final paragraph should say what action you think should be taken by the person to whom you are writing.
- You should include a polite sentence to end the letter.

Instructions for tasks 1–3

- Key in your address and date at the right margin using the right align button.
- Key in the address of the person to whom you are writing at the left margin.
- Key in the letter at the left margin.
- At the end, use 'Yours sincerely' if the letter begins with a name (such as 'Dear Mrs Jones'). Use 'Yours faithfully' if the letter begins with 'Dear Sir or Madam'.

Section 9 – tasks 1 to 3

Task 1

COMPLAINT

You have been on a visit to the cinema. You did not enjoy the film, because your seat was uncomfortable.

Write a letter of complaint to the manager of the cinema and ask him or her for your money back.

Task 2

QUESTION

You have just finished reading an exciting book. It was so good that you would like to buy another book just like it.

Write a letter to the publisher of the book and ask if there are any more books like this one that you can buy.

Task 3

THANK YOU

You have been on a school trip to a wildlife park. You really enjoyed yourself and could hardly bear to come home!

Write a letter to the manager of the park to say how much you enjoyed your visit and that you would like to go back again very soon.

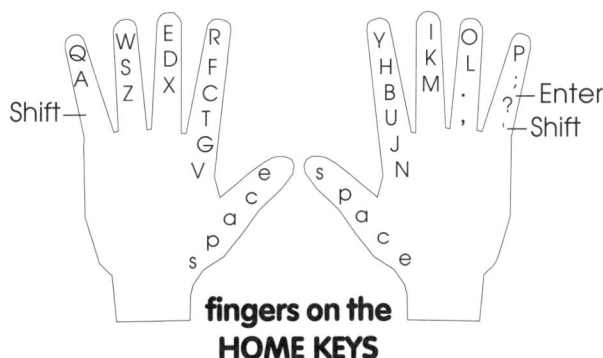

fingers on the HOME KEYS

Section 10
Correction signs

Sign in margin	Meaning		Sign in text
⌒⟩	delete text		The cat ~~sat~~ on the mat.
∿∿∿	change to bold		The cat sat on the mat.
————	change to italics		The cat <u>sat</u> on the mat.
⟨under⟩	underline		The cat (sat) on the mat.
⟨centre⟩	centre	(use the words 'left' and 'right' to align the text at the left or right margins)	⟨The cat sat on the mat.⟩
≡	change to capital letters		The cat <u>sat</u> on the mat.
≠	change to lower case letters		The cat <u>SAT</u> on the mat.
#⟨	insert a space		The cat sat on⟨the mat.
⌢	delete a space		The cat sat on ⌢ the mat.
|−|⟨	insert a hyphen		The cat sat on the cat⟨mat.
|n|⟨	insert a dash	(called an 'n' dash because it is the same width as a letter n)	The cat sat⟨on the mat.
//	start a new paragraph		The cat sat//The dog ran.
⟶	join two paragraphs		The cat sat.⟶ ⌐The dog ran.

Instructions for Section 10

Using the correction signs
- The chart above shows the most common correction signs. These are the signs used by publishers and printers to correct text.
- These signs should be written on text that needs to be corrected.
- If you need to make a correction but you do not know the sign, write a short note in the margin to explain what needs to be done.

Instructions for tasks 1 and 2
- **Note:** there are deliberate mistakes in tasks 1 and 2, but you must key in exactly what you see.
- Look at the correction signs chart and make the changes.
- Proof-read your work, correct any errors.
- Print a copy of your work.

Section 10 – task 1 (sheet 1)

Key in exactly what you see.

The Milky Way

This is our own galaxy. It consists of a hundredmillion stars. there are many millions of galaxies in the universe.

Sightings of UFOs

There are 40 reported sightings of UFOs every day. In the last   30 years, 100,000 people have reported seeing a UFO.

Aliens

Many people suspect that there is life in outer space. There have been many films about aliens and many people have ideas about what aliens might look like, but no one has actually seen one or have they?

Astronauts and cosmonauts

'Astronaut' comes from Latin and Greek words meaning 'star sailor'. The Russian word for 'astronaut' is 'cosmonaut', which means 'sailor of the universe'.

Meteoroid

Meteoroids are lumps of rock that fly around in space. Sometimes these rocks are pulled towards the Earth by gravity, but mostly they burn up before hitting the surface of the Earth.

Changes

Carry out the editing as marked on sheet 2.

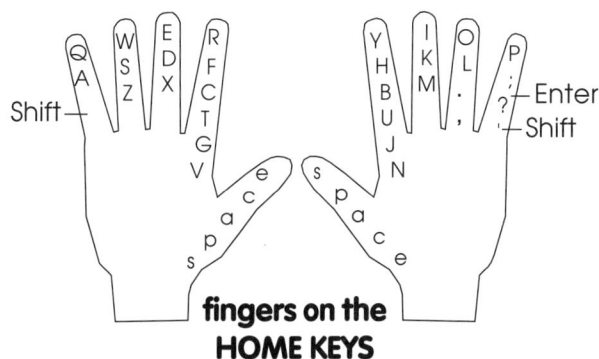

fingers on the
HOME KEYS

Section 10 – task 1 (sheet 2)

The Milky Way

This is our own galaxy. It consists of a hundred million stars. there are many millions of galaxies in the universe.

Sightings of UFOs

There are 40 reported sightings of UFOs every day. In the last 30 years, 100,000 people have reported seeing a UFO.

Aliens

Many people suspect that there is life in outer space. There have been many films about aliens and many people have ideas about what aliens might look like, but no one has actually seen one or have they?

Astronauts and cosmonauts

'Astronaut' comes from Latin and Greek words meaning 'star sailor'. The Russian word for 'astronaut' is 'cosmonaut', which means 'sailor of the universe'.

under

Meteoroid

Meteoroids are lumps of rock that fly around in space. Sometimes these rocks are pulled towards the Earth by gravity, but mostly they burn up before hitting the surface of the Earth.

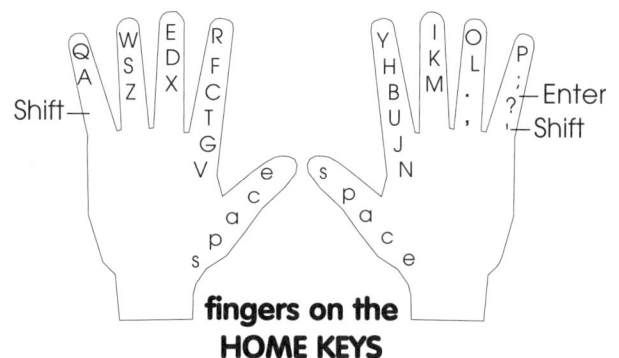

Shift —

fingers on the
HOME KEYS

Section 10 – task 2 (sheet 1)

Key in exactly what you see.

Talismans and amulets

Talismans and amulets are both different kinds of mascot. A talisman is a mascot that brings good luck and wards off danger. An amulet is a mascot that protects the person that carries it.

Originally, amulets were carried to ward off evil spirits. Talismans were worn to cure illnesses and bring riches and love.

Many people throughout history have believed in the power of talismans and amulets. These mascots are often made using onyx, amber and coral beads (to protect the wearer from evil), blue beads (for luck in love) and jet beads (for hope and success).

Charms and symbols

Crosses have been worn for many years. One of the oldest crosses is the Tau Cross. It is in the shape of a large letter T. This cross is worn as an amulet to protect against disease and evil spirits.

The most well-known use of the cross, of course, is as a symbol of Christianity. Other religions also have their own symbols and charms.

For example, Sikhs have the Khanda symbol, which appears on flags outside Sikh temples. The symbol includes a double-edged sword to show the almighty power of God.

There are many more charms of different kinds, such as horseshoes, wishbones, keys and four-leaf clovers. People all over the world use these charms in many different ways and for many different reasons.

Changes

Carry out the editing as marked on sheet 2.

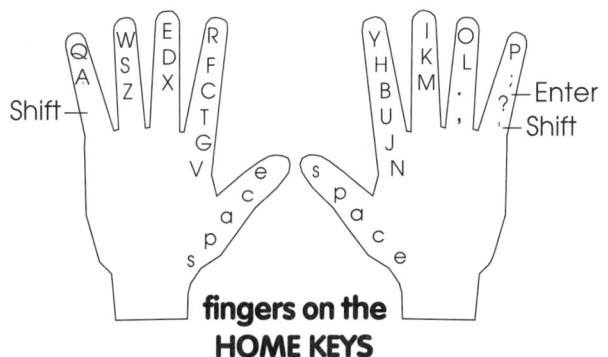

fingers on the HOME KEYS

Section 10 – task 2 (sheet 2)

Talismans and amulets   (centre)

Talismans and amulets are both different kinds of mascot. A talisman is a mascot that brings good luck and wards off danger. An amulet is a mascot that protects the person that carries it.

Originally, amulets were carried to ward off evil spirits. Talismans were worn to cure illnesses and bring riches and love.

Many people throughout history have believed in the power of talismans and amulets. These mascots are often made using onyx, amber and coral beads (to protect the wearer from evil), blue beads (for luck in love) and jet beads (for hope and success).

Charms and symbols   (centre)

Crosses have been worn for many years. One of the oldest crosses is the Tau Cross. It is in the shape of a large letter T. This cross is worn as an amulet to protect against disease and evil spirits.

The most well-known use of the cross, of course, is as a symbol of Christianity. Other religions also have their own symbols and charms.

For example, Sikhs have the Khanda symbol, which appears on flags outside Sikh temples. The symbol includes a double-edged sword to show the almighty power of God.

There are many more charms of different kinds, such as horseshoes, wishbones, keys and four-leaf clovers//People all over the world use these charms in many different ways and for many different reasons.

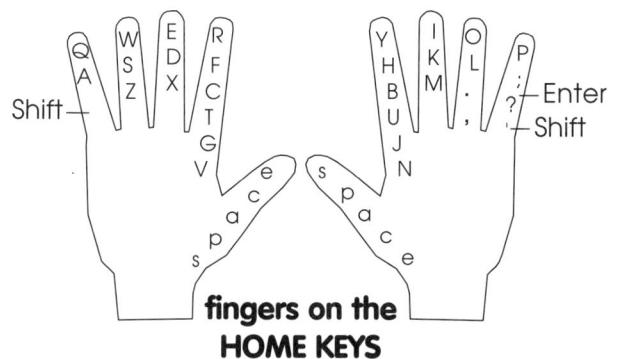

Shift — Enter
— Shift

fingers on the HOME KEYS

Section 11
Additional facilities

To view your document before printing
- Click on **File** in the menu bar.
- Click on **Print Preview**.
- Use the page up/ page down key to view more than one page.
- Press the escape key to close print preview.

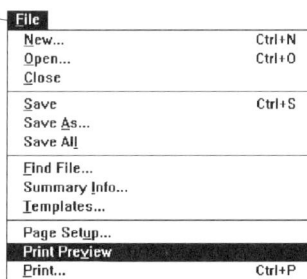

To check the spelling in your document
- Place the cursor at the beginning of your text.
- Click on the spelling button.
- A box will appear and show words that the computer does not recognise.

- Click on **Ignore** if you do not want the word to change. Click on **Change** if you want to insert the new word.
- Press the escape key to close spell check.
- Remember to use the spell check only as a final check. You should make sure that you are spelling words correctly as you key them in!

To insert a page break
- When you type in a large amount of text, an automatic page break will appear when you reach the bottom of the page.
- However, it is bad presentation to allow this automatic page break to appear in the middle of a sentence. Change the page break so that it comes above or below the last sentence.
- Place the cursor at the beginning of the sentence. Hold down the control key and press the enter/return key. A page break will appear above the sentence.

---------------------------------Page Break---------------------------------

- To remove a page break, place the cursor under the break and press the delete key.

To change the margins
- Click on **File** in the menu bar.
- Click on **Page Setup**.
- A box will appear showing the size of each margin.
- Change the margins to the size you want, but try to leave at least 2cm all the way around the page.

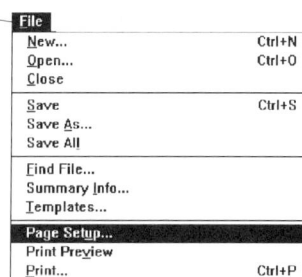

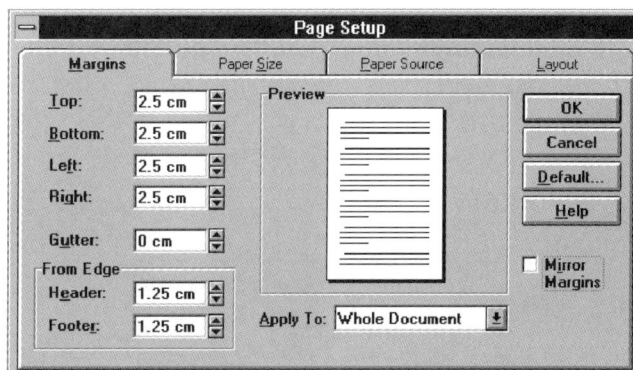

Section 11
Additional facilities

To replace or change a word throughout your document

- Go to the beginning of the document.
- Click on **Edit** in the menu bar.
- Click on **Replace**.
- A box will appear. Key in the word you want to find and then the word you want to replace it with.
- For example, if you want to replace the word 'monster' with the word 'ghost', key in 'monster' in the first space and 'ghost' in the second space.
- Click on **Replace All** to change the word throughout your document.

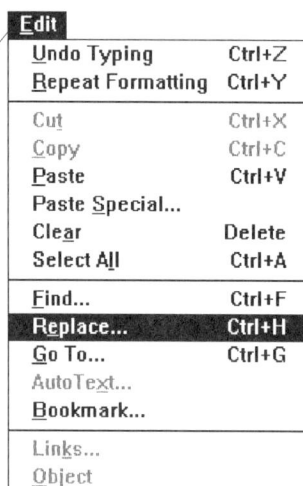

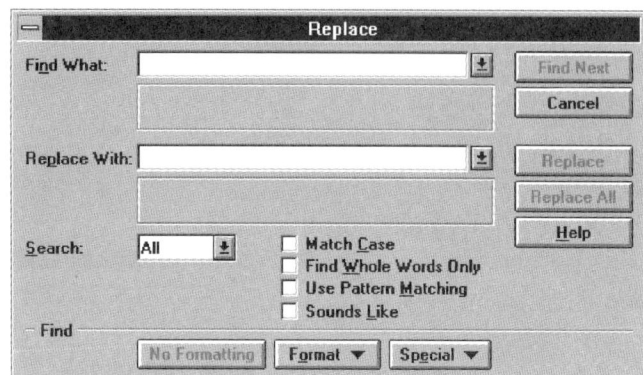

Edit

Undo Typing	Ctrl+Z
Repeat Formatting	Ctrl+Y
Cut	Ctrl+X
Copy	Ctrl+C
Paste	Ctrl+V
Paste Special...	
Clear	Delete
Select All	Ctrl+A
Find...	Ctrl+F
Replace...	Ctrl+H
Go To...	Ctrl+G
AutoText...	
Bookmark...	
Links...	
Object	

Replace

Find What:

Replace With:

Search: All

- Match Case
- Find Whole Words Only
- Use Pattern Matching
- Sounds Like

Find Next / Cancel / Replace / Replace All / Help

Find

No Formatting / Format ▼ / Special ▼

To insert bullets or numbers, or indent a whole paragraph

- Highlight the paragraph to be changed, then click on the button you need from the toolbar.

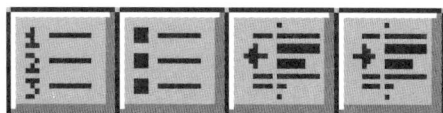

To insert symbols

- Place the cursor in the position in your document where you want your symbol to appear.
- Click on **Insert**.
- Click on **Symbol**.
- A box will appear with a table of symbols. You can choose different tables of symbols by clicking on the arrow at the top of the box.
- Click anywhere on the grid and then use the arrow keys to move around the grid. Each symbol will be enlarged when you move the cursor on to it.
- When you have found the symbol you want, click on **Insert**. The symbol will appear in your document, where you have placed the cursor.

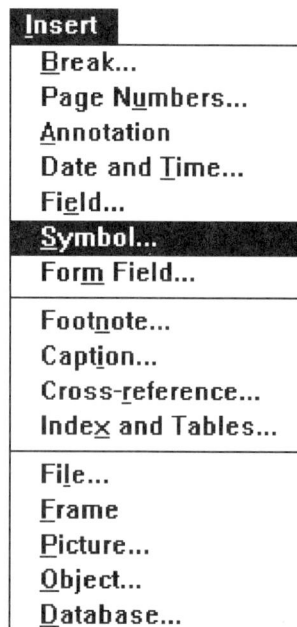

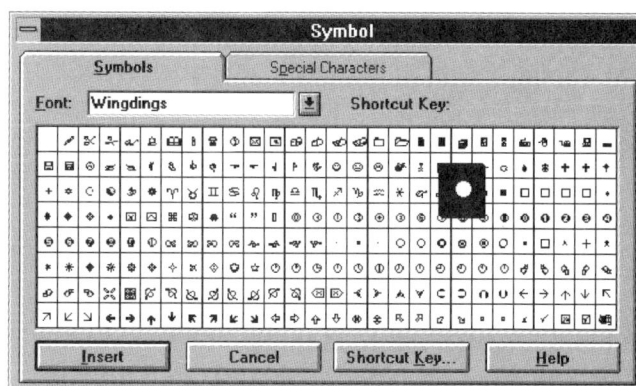

Insert

- Break...
- Page Numbers...
- Annotation
- Date and Time...
- Field...
- Symbol...
- Form Field...
- Footnote...
- Caption...
- Cross-reference...
- Index and Tables...
- File...
- Frame
- Picture...
- Object...
- Database...

Symbol

Symbols / Special Characters

Font: Wingdings   Shortcut Key:

Insert / Cancel / Shortcut Key... / Help

- When you have finished inserting symbols, click on **Close**.
- You could make your symbol larger by highlighting it and then choosing a higher number from the ribbon.

Section 11
Additional facilities

Customising your documents

- Altering the size of the print, using bold, italics and underline are all ways of customising your text.
- Changing the line spacing, indenting certain paragraphs and using capital letters for headings all add interest to text, making it eye-catching.
- Symbols can be used to decorate posters, covers of projects, and so on.

Adding borders and shading

> - Another way of making a heading or a piece of text stand out is by adding a border.

> - Using shading also makes the text stand out. This is done after keying in the text, as part of the editing process.

- To add a border, highlight the text to be changed, then click on **Format**.
- Click on **Borders and Shading**.
- A box will appear. Click on **Borders** at the top of the box.

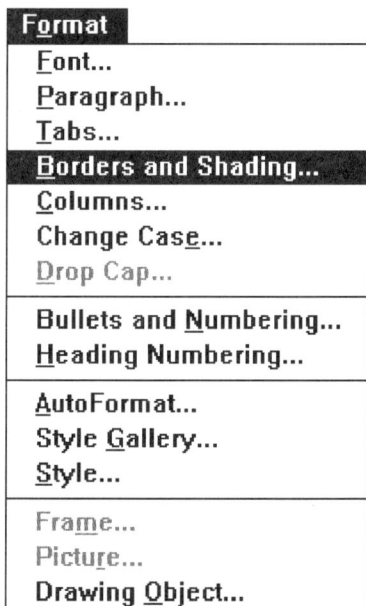

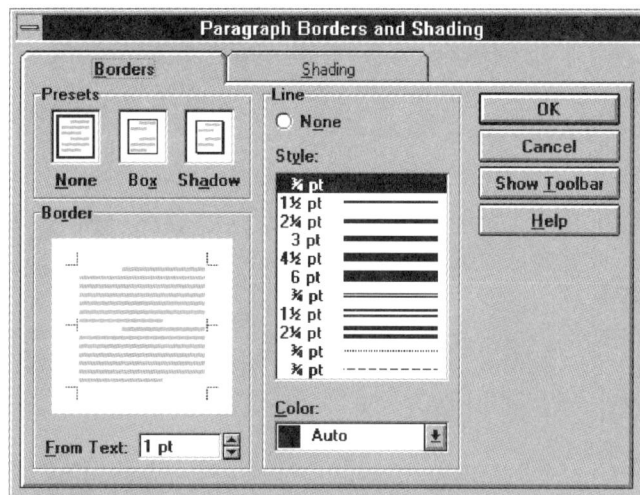

Format
- Font...
- Paragraph...
- Tabs...
- **Borders and Shading...**
- Columns...
- Change Case...
- Drop Cap...
- Bullets and Numbering...
- Heading Numbering...
- AutoFormat...
- Style Gallery...
- Style...
- Frame...
- Picture...
- Drawing Object...

Paragraph Borders and Shading

Borders | Shading

Presets: None, Box, Shadow

Line: None
Style:
½ pt
1½ pt
2¼ pt
3 pt
4½ pt
6 pt
¾ pt
1½ pt
2¼ pt
¾ pt
¾ pt

Color: Auto

Border

From Text: 1 pt

OK | Cancel | Show Toolbar | Help

- Click on the style of line you would like to use for your border.
- To add shading, click on **Shading** at the top of the box.
- If you do not want shading, click on **OK**. The border will appear in your document.

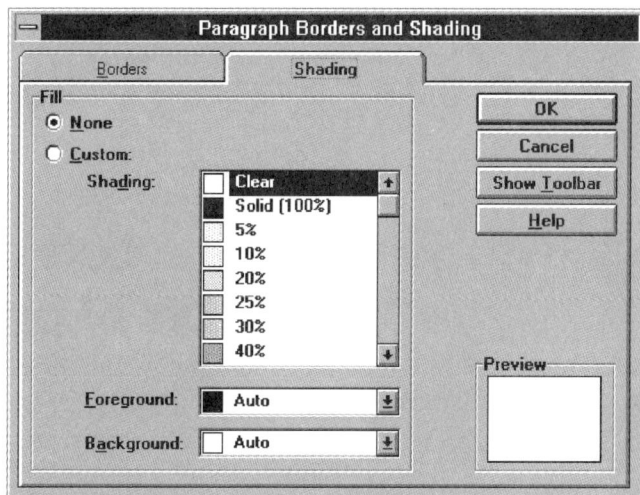

Paragraph Borders and Shading

Borders | Shading

Fill
- None
- Custom:

Shading:
Clear
Solid (100%)
5%
10%
20%
25%
30%
40%

Foreground: Auto
Background: Auto

Preview

OK | Cancel | Show Toolbar | Help

- Click on the style of shading you would like for your text.
- Remember to be careful when using shading – if the shading is too dark, you will not be able to read your text.
- Click on **OK**. The shading will appear in your document.

FOLENS IT – *Keyboard Skills Book 3*

Section 11 – task 1

- Produce a poster like this to advertise your school Christmas party.
- Use borders, shading and symbols to decorate your poster.

❋❋❋❋❋❋❋❋❋❋❋❋   — 20 point

School
Christmas Party   — 30 point

16 DECEMBER   — 20 point

✳ ✳ ✳ ✳ ✳   — 20 point

**In the Main Hall
6.00pm–8.00pm**   — 20 point

❋❋❋   — 20 point

**Lots of food!
Lots of party games!**   — 20 point + border

**RAFFLE
FATHER CHRISTMAS
PANTOMIME**   — 20 point + border + 10% shading

❋❋❋❋❋❋❋❋❋   — 20 point